Write! Social Studies

Multiple Intelligences & Cooperative Learning Writing Activities

Virginia DeBolt

Kagan

Kagan Publishing
981 Calle Amanecer
San Clemente, CA 92673
1(800) 933-2667
www.KaganOnline.com

ISBN: 978-1-879097-40-7

Table of Contents

Virginia DeBolt: *Write! Social Studies*
Kagan Publishing • 1 (800) 933-2667

I

Table of Contents

Journal Topic Chart

You will find Journal Topics on pages:

29, 33, 37, 45, 51, 55, 71, 91, 110

Virginia DeBolt: *Write! Social Studies*
Kagan Publishing • 1 (800) 933-2667

Chart of Structures

	Basic Description	See Also Activities
Agreement Circles	112	22
Blind Sequencing	113	18
Find-the-Fiction	114	34
Jigsaw Problem Solving	115	4, 9
Pair Discussion	116	17, 19
Pair Project	116	5, 11, 26, 29, 32
Pairs Compare	117	33
Pairs Present	117	11, 26
RallyTable	118	17
RoundRobin	118	1, 2, 3, 4, 5, 6, 7, 8, 9, 10, 13, 14, 17,19, 21, 22, 23, 24, 25, 27, 28, 29, 30, 31, 33,
RoundTable	119	35, 36
Teams Post	120	15, 21
Stand-N-Share	120	24
Team Discussion	121	14
Team Interview	121	14, 24
Team Project	122	4, 12
Teams Present	123	3, 13, 18, 20, 27, 34
ThinkPad Brainstorming	124	3, 9, 10, 13, 20, 27
Think-Pair-Share	125	6, 10
Think-Pair-Write	126	8, 11, 25
Think-Write-Pair	127	30
Think-Write-Pair-Square	128	2, 23
Value Line	129	16

Virginia DeBolt: *Write! Social Studies*
Kagan Publishing • 1 (800) 933-2667

III

Acknowledgements

Many people at Kagan Publishing worked with me to bring this book to completion. Thank you to Dr. Spencer Kagan for his continuing support and assistance, to Miguel Kagan for overseeing the details of putting this book into its present form, to Karen Schumacher and Catherine Hurlbert for formatting the book, and to Celso Rodriguez for creating the art.

Virginia DeBolt: *Write! Social Studies*
Kagan Publishing • 1 (800) 933-2667

Part I

Integrating Writing and Social Studies

"Countless careers rise or fall on the ability or inability of employees to state a set of facts, summarize a meeting or present an idea coherently."

–William Zinsser

Today's teachers are encouraged to include writing in all the subject areas, including social studies. Writing during social studies or in the social studies classroom may feel foreign at first. Events, dates and terminology are perceived to be the language of social studies. However, integrating writing in science enhances and improves students' understanding of social studies. Writing is a tool for learning in social studies as surely as a time line or a map. Teachers can use writing as part of daily instruction. Students can use writing in social studies, not as a novelist or poet would use writing, but the way a social scientist would use writing.

To write is to compose. To compose well is to comprehend. Writing is not speaking, where we hope that the, ahh, listeners, like, you know, get it. Writing demands careful word choice, clear thinking, complete communication. The physical act of writing takes longer than thinking or speaking, and so seems to allow the brain time for the discoveries and connections writers often make while writing. Professional writers, when asked to explain why they write, often answer that they write to find out what they're thinking, what they know and what it means. As students write, they develop their knowledge of a subject. They discover, organize, classify, connect and evaluate information.

Integrating writing and social studies moves students beyond the basic facts of social studies. Writing allows students to look critically and creatively at social studies, enriching students'

Writing to Learn	vs.	**Reading to Learn**
What do you have to say?		What did they have to say?
Be active. Do it.		Sit still. Pay attention.
Student chooses the words.		Teacher chooses the words.
Productive. Output.		Consumptive. Input.

Virginia DeBolt: *Write! Social Studies*
Kagan Publishing • 1 (800) 933-2667

1

understanding and appreciation of social studies. By writing about social studies, students are doing the work a true social scientist; learning becomes more real and more meaningful. As you integrate writing and social studies, think of it as an enhancement to teaching social studies rather than as one more thing to cram into an already crowded curriculum.

Indeed, writing is a terrific tool for teaching social studies as well as the other disciplines, but it is more than that. Writing is a life skill, highly valued by society. Writing is everywhere. Every aspect of human endeavor needs writing about—how else would we pass along the information? The box below is a partial list of things people write or write about. Notice how diverse the writings are.

This list is not at all complete. Wander through the nonfiction stacks in your library. People write about everything. Most writing today is nonfiction, and the need for nonfiction writers continues to grow. Expanding technology in an information age demands it. Nonfiction has never been so important. We are building our national future on information and writers are in demand to explain it. We live in a wired world where communication is essential. Writing across the curriculum gives students the ability to think and communicate today and tomorrow.

So, What Do I Need to Know About Writing?

Enough about the rationale for integrating writing. You're probably reading this book now because you're already convinced about the value of writing. So what do you need to know? The first thing you and your students should know about writing is that

What We Write About

- advertisements
- agendas
- animal medicine
- animals
- annotated calendars
- art
- autobiographies
- awards and inscriptions
- biographies
- biology
- business
- captions and labels
- cartoons
- case studies

- chemistry
- coin new words
- collecting
- computer programs
- concerts
- constellations
- contest entries
- dance
- diaries and journals
- drug abuse
- e mail
- economics
- editorials and opinions
- essays

- eulogies
- fashion
- features
- field guides
- field journals
- film
- folk remedies
- folk traditions
- folklore
- foreign language journaling
- forms
- games and puzzles
- geography
- history

Virginia DeBolt: *Write! Social Studies*
Kagan Publishing • 1 (800) 933-2667

10 Rules for Writers

1. Write.
2. Write.
3. Write Often.
4. Write about anything.
5. Write about everything.
6. Write about what you see.
7. Write about what you learn.
8. Write about what you think.
9. Write about what you read.
10. WRITE!

there are 10 rules to writing that are absolutely critical. See the 10 Rules at left. These 10 rules are a way to emphasize that the road to becoming a better writer (and social scientist) is to write, write, and write some more! Use these 10 rules as a handout or overhead as you describe the use of writing to your students (see page 14).

The next thing about writing you and your students should know is that writing is considered a process—the Writing Process. This process includes prewriting, revising, editing, proofreading and publishing. Publishing is not necessarily a "publication." Publishing could be reading work aloud to the class, posting work on a bulletin board, polishing an essay to turn in to the teacher or other types of sharing. Teaching students to move about in the process of writing is often considered as important as the final written product.

The writing process is not linear. It is a circular process. At any point, students can confer, evaluate, and rewrite. For that reason, the writing process is put in a wheel with Conferring/Evaluating/Rewriting in the center of the wheel (see page 15).

The activities in this book focus heavily on the prewriting and writing stages of the process. We've already covered writing, what's so important about prewriting? It's the time when concepts form, vocabulary develops, ideas grow from the synergy of interaction with other students. Prewriting is a social act. Students talk, banter, give and receive feedback. Prewriting develops the readiness to write. Prewriting primes the pump from which the writing will pour.

In the activities in this book, students discuss, plan, outline and brainstorm cooperatively before

What We Write About

- humor
- instructions and advice
- interactive media
- interviews
- learning logs
- lists and notes
- literature
- medicine
- memoirs
- memoranda and messages
- mottoes and slogans
- music
- mythology
- nature

- news stories
- office business
- oral histories
- parodies
- petitions
- philosophy
- physics
- public notices
- recipes
- reports of current events
- research reports
- resumes and cover letters
- reviews
- rules and regulations

- scrapbooks
- simulations
- song lyrics
- sports
- technology
- telegrams
- textbooks
- thumbnail sketches
- time capsule lists
- travel

Virginia DeBolt: *Write! Social Studies*
Kagan Publishing • 1 (800) 933-2667

they actually do any writing. The reason is because prewriting makes writing easier and better. Writers will tell you that they are always writing. A composition of words swirls inside the brain no matter what else a writer might appear to be doing. When a writer sits down to write, it may seem that the words flow easily, when actually considerable time was spent on the words already.

Since most students will not be rehearsing compositions during their spare moments, you can improve the quality of what students write by providing ample time for prewriting activities. As a rule of thumb, the more time you allow for prewriting, the better the writing will be. Therefore, if you draw from only one aspect of the writing process, let it be prewriting.

But prewriting and writing are not the whole story for integrating writing and social studies. Consider these examples: *Lives of a Cell* by Lewis Thomas, *Silent Spring* by Rachel Carson, *Voyage of the Beagle* by Charles Darwin, *The Immense Journey* by Loren Eisley. These books contain some of the most powerful and beautiful language ever written. Like all good writing, these books were not just written. They were revised, proofread, carefully edited, and finally published, to be shared with others.

Sharing and publishing are extremely important parts of the writing process, not to be overlooked. By sharing, students can learn from each other what good writing looks and sounds like. Since the writing is about social studies, students become their own Social studies teachers as they share their learning, connections and reflections.

Many activities include a sharing component. You can easily have students read any of their writing to a partner, to teammates, or even to the entire class. Students can also share their writing by exchanging papers or by posting their papers in a location where classmates can read them. Sharing and publishing make writing a learning experience not only for the writer, but for the recipient as well.

Peer Editing and Conferencing

The social studies writing activities in this book focus primarily on using writing as a means to teach social studies. The emphasis is more on the content than the writing itself. However, with a little work, any writing assignment can be easily turned into a polished work of art. What do you do when students need to revise, proofread and edit? Let students help each other. Establish small groups for peer editing and conferencing.

Students offer each other valuable ideas about writing. Since students identify with the words they write and can be

Virginia DeBolt: *Write! Social Studies*
Kagan Publishing • 1 (800) 933-2667

Peer Conference Gambit Cards

Directions: Cut out the cards below. Use these sentence starters when you respond to writing.

I like the part where...

I like the way you used the word _____.

What did you mean when you said...

What happened after...

I liked your beginning because...

I would like to know more about...

I had a clear picture in my mind of the part where...

What would you lose if...

What are you going to do next?

Peer Conference Response Form

Author's Name _____
Title _____
Helper's Name _____
Date _____

I like

I want to know more about

One thing you might think about doing

Other

Peer Response | Title _____
Name _____

Rough Draft

eternally wounded by thoughtless critical comments, your task is to keep the conferences positive. Because students can sometimes be masters of the outspoken insult, it helps to establish a few basic rules for peer conferences, such as:

- Begin with positive comments about what is good in the writing.

- Ask questions that help the writer discover ways to change writing for the better, like:

"I don't understand, could you explain this part a little more?"

"Do you think it would help to change the order of these paragraphs?"

"Would you like for me to underline the words I think you've spelled wrong?"

- Remember that the writer is the final judge of how the writing should be changed.

As a peer conference technique, teaching students to ask questions about another's writing works well. The questions become an indicator of where the writing needs to be changed and improved. There are fewer hurt feelings and arguments because the writers learn what doesn't work in their writing without hearing comments such as, "That third paragraph really stinks—throw it out."

It will help students maintain a positive attitude toward each other if you brainstorm with them to develop a list of ways to say things

that help without hurt or insult. Ask them, "How would you like to be told that your writing was disorganized or unclear?" Post their ideas for easy viewing.

In the back of this chapter, you will find a number of forms that will be helpful for peer editing and conferencing. On page 16, there is a Proofreader's Marks form. Have students use these standard marks as they edit each other's papers. For consistency, use them yourself as you edit students' papers.

On page 17 there are gambit cards for students to use in peer conferences. These gambit cards are sentence starters for students as they have peer conferences. They direct the conference and promote a positive tone.

The Peer Conference Response Form on page 18 is another form helpful for peer conferences. Have students fill out their response form before the peer conference, then students go over their comments together.

Page 19 is a Peer Response Form. Students write in the lined space provided. When done, they give it to a peer to respond to the writing in the left margin. They then meet to go over the responses.

What About Grading?
A writing assignment will sink into quicksand if students think they won't be graded. The type of grading you do largely depends on

Virginia DeBolt: *Write! Social Studies*
Kagan Publishing • 1 (800) 933-2667

5

the type and frequency of writing assignments students do. I suggest an on-going, long-term approach to writing and grading, using writing journals and a writing portfolio. We will look at both journals and portfolios in depth after some general comments on grading.

The first comment on grading is: Don't make grading too labor-intensive for yourself to limit the frequency and volume of student writing. The more students write, the more they learn. More writing also means more grading and more work for you, right? Not necessarily. If you have unlimited time and energy, grade and respond to every writing assignment. If not, grade everything but don't read everything. Yes, grade everything but don't read everything. Students need to know that everything they write might be read, but that doesn't mean you have to read everything. We'll examine this idea in more detail in the sections on journals and portfolios.

The second general comment on grading is: Align your grading practices with the type of writing students do. Glance through the journal topics and activities in this book. You will see a range of writing assignments. You should use a different grading approach depending on the type of writing.

Writing assignments that check for understanding should be turned in for immediate response while the topic is still fresh. Elaborate writing assignments like reports and final papers require individual attention, feedback and usually impact a student's course grade. With most other activities and journal writings, the process of writing and sharing is more important than the evaluation. Students can save these assignments for periodic journal and portfolio checks.

A multipronged approach to grading allows the teacher to hold students accountable for even the most frequent writing assignments, yet at the same time, makes it unnecessary for the teacher to read every word the student writes.

Writing Journals

Some writing might be done in a daily journal. A spiral-bound notebook is a nice way to keep all journal writing assignments together.

Good journal topics are reusable.
- Write for five minutes about yesterday's homework.
- Tell everything you learned about _____ today.
- What did you miss on the test? Do you know it now?
- Summarize last night's reading assignment.
- We are beginning a new chapter. Write everything you already know about it. Tell what you want to know about it.

Virginia DeBolt: *Write! Social Studies*
Kagan Publishing • 1 (800) 933-2667

• Write about the hardest or most confusing part of _____ _____ .

Journals can be easily individualized. Students who benefit from the use of clusters and mind maps might use the left pages for that and the right pages for writing. Students who learn or remember with pictures and symbols can incorporate visuals in their journal. Quotes from the text might be written on one side of a page, and the student's response to the quotes on the other. Journal writing is private, although it may be shared with classmates and will be shared with the teacher. Nevertheless, it is a student's personal record of growth, progress, learning, and individual revelations about personal learning styles and successes.

You will find Journal Topics on pages:

29, 33, 37, 45, 51, 55, 71, 91, 110

You will find Journal Topics scattered throughout the activities section of this book. For quick reference, see the Journal Topics chart at left.

A check, check minus or check plus may be used to check for the quality of writing. If you don't have the time to read all journals, use a plus or minus in your grade book to indicate whether or not a student has completed each journal assignment. To keep up with journals on a daily basis, I suggest that in each period you collect,

read and respond to three journals In ten days, (two weeks) you will have read thirty students' journals. Read only the journal entry from the day you collect the journal, but do a quick flip-through to be sure the student is writing all the assignments. Reading and responding to three journal entries a day should take no more than five minutes. Journals can be returned to the students or to a storage area immediately.

To respond to a journal entry, simply read it and write a quick response. The teacher is rather like a pen pal, exchanging ideas informally with the writer. What sort of response do you make to a journal entry? Ask a question designed to make the student dig deeper. Give a helpful comment that might clear up a problem. Give praise for good thinking. Focus on the academic subject under consideration. One good question or comment is enough. What your response really does is tell the student that his or her learning process is important to you, that you consider it worth recording and reflecting upon, and that the student is a major participant in his or her own learning.

Writing Portfolio

Have students keep their writing activities from this book in a three-ring binder. This collection of writing activities serves as a writing portfolio. Students need to know that writing they do will

Virginia DeBolt: *Write! Social Studies*
Kagan Publishing • 1 (800) 933-2667

7

be graded somehow, even if it's just for completeness, and that you have a serious commitment to that part of your curriculum. You can grade the material in the binder periodically, perhaps every six weeks.

A more differentiated approach to grading portfolios may include developing a workable grading matrix based on requirements such as completeness, organization, appearance, or other criteria you consider important. You may ask students to provide a table of contents, index, tabs and other helpful aids in their binder. The writing portfolio becomes a record of what the students have learned as well as how students' writing has developed over time. In addition to using the portfolio for grading, have students use it as a tool for reflection about their progress in writing and learning in social studies.

Using the Writing Activities

In this book you'll find a variety of types of writing activities such as: writing that enables the student to reflect on his or her thinking; writing that enables the student to remember, clarify, and connect new learning to previous knowledge; writing that augments classroom discussions and activities; writing that lets the teacher see into the student's thought processes; and writing that demonstrates learning to a specified audience.

Many of the writing activities in this book are general, and intentionally so. Because curriculum varies from grade-to-grade and class-to-class, these activities were designed as close to "one size fits all" as possible.

For specific content applications of the activity, see the Idea Bank in each activity for a number of ideas. There is also space under More Ideas for My Class for you to fill in ideas to use the activity with your own curriculum. As you read the activity, make sure to fill in additional ideas. That way, when you begin a topic or unit you can flip through the activities to find the ones that will apply.

Many of the activities can be used meaningfully more than once with new content. Some you may find yourself returning to time and time again.

Between the activities, the journal topics, the ideas for my class, and your own writing ideas, you should have more than enough writing topics and activities to integrate writing into your social studies curriculum all year long.

The writing activities you'll find in this book were designed to incorporate three progressive movements in education: cooperative learning, multiple intelligences, and higher-level thinking. Let's take a quick look at each innovation and how each are included in these activities. We will briefly examine Dr. Spencer

Virginia DeBolt: *Write! Social Studies*
Kagan Publishing • 1 (800) 933-2667

8

Kagan's 6 Key Concepts

1. Teams
2. Will
3. Management
4. Skills
5. Basic Principles
6. Structures

Kagan's approach to cooperative learning, Howard Gardner's theory of multiple intelligences, and Benjamin Bloom's taxonomy of thinking.

Cooperative Learning

Research has found that cooperative learning promotes higher achievement than competitive and individualistic learning structures across all age levels, subject areas, and almost all tasks. Writing and science are no exceptions!

Cooperative learning is a natural partner of writing. Cooperative work provides a place for students to brainstorm ideas, develop language and vocabulary, get constructive feedback, and share final works.

Small group interaction provides students with a less threatening environment in which to share their writing and gives every student an equal opportunity to be an active participant throughout the stages of the writing process. An at-risk student, who may have given up on class participation in a whole class structure, is "hooked in" to small group processes and becomes a contributor rather than a distracter.

Cooperative groups supply the teacher with a positive method of channeling the energy to socialize and interact into productive work.

The activities in this book focus on Dr. Spencer Kagan's approach to cooperative learning. For more details on the theory, research and application of cooperative learning, see Dr. Kagan's popular and comprehensive book, *Kagan Cooperative Learning*, available from Kagan Publishing.

In his book, Dr. Kagan outlines six key concepts helpful for making cooperative learning a success in the class. (See box at left.) Many of these key concepts are integrated into the activities in this book, especially the cooperative learning structures. The activities in this book work well as stand-alone cooperative events, but work even better in a cooperative classroom environment. Kagan's six keys to cooperative learning are as follows:

1. Teams

A team is a small group of students who work together. For these activities, teams of four are ideal. They are small enough for active participation and split evenly for equal participation during pair work. Teams should be carefully selected by the teacher to reflect a mixture of ability levels, gender and ethnicity. Teams should stay together for approximately six weeks.

2. Will

For cooperative learning to run successfully, students must have the will to cooperate. Classbuilding and teambuilding activities give students the opportunity

Virginia DeBolt: *Write! Social Studies*
Kagan Publishing • 1 (800) 933-2667

9

to interact with teammates and classmates in a positive way and promote an environment conducive to successful teamwork and create a positive class atmosphere. There are three great activity books available from Kagan Publishing that I can recommend to create the "Will" to cooperate: *Classbuilding, Teambuilding,* and *Communitybuilding.*

3. Management

A number of cooperative management tools helps the teacher run the cooperative classroom more effectively. Kagan describes a host of management tools including using a quiet signal, assigning roles, using modeling, team questions, and more.

4. Skills

Students need social skills such as listening, conflict resolution, and tutoring to work together successfully. Social skills can be taught directly, but with some direction, many can be naturally acquired in the context of cooperative learning.

5. Basic Principles

The are four basic principles to successful cooperative learning summarized by the acronym PIES: **P**ositive Interdependence, **I**ndividual Accountability, **E**qual Participation and **S**imultaneous Interaction. The box at right illustrates the four basic principles and the critical question associated with each principle.

Positive Interdependence

Kagan defines positive interdependence as, "Two individuals are positively interdependent if the gains of either helps the other…Strong Positive Interdependence is created when a student cannot make a gain without a gain of another student. Weak Positive Interdependence is created when a gain for one may produce a gain for another, but it is not *necessary* (italics added)." Students are positively interdependent as they work together to help each other with their writing and learning.

Individual Accountability

Individual Accountability means that each student is responsible for and graded on his or her own learning, contribution, and performance. A student might be held accountable for helping another student learn a new skill in a Pairs Check activity. A student might be held accountable for listening in a Paraphrase activity. A student might be held accountable for learning by passing a test. Most activities have an independent writing component that can be used to hold students accountable for sharing or turning in.

Equal Participation

Equal Participation means that each student has an equal chance to speak, to read, to offer answers and to think. Guarantee Equal Participation by structuring activities so that

PIES
The Principles of Cooperative Learning

Is a gain for one, a gain for another? Is help necessary?

Is individual public performance required?

How equal is the participation?

What percent are overtly active at once?

Virginia DeBolt: *Write! Social Studies*
Kagan Publishing • 1 (800) 933-2667

10

everyone must participate. Assigning roles is one way to accomplish this. If each person has a job to do, each person is participating. Equal Participation can also be created by using turn taking and turn-taking structures. Turn-taking structures include RoundRobin, RoundTable, RallyRobin, RallyTable, Think-Pair-Share, Three-Step Interview and Pairs Check.

Simultaneous Interaction

Simultaneous Interaction gives you and your students the gift of time. Time for students to read their writing aloud. Time for language development during prewriting. Time for students to manage their own revising and editing when necessary.

How does Simultaneous Interaction give you time? Suppose, for example, that the students have written about the most difficult aspect of their last homework assignment. Having each student share with the class for one minute would take over half an hour. Instead, by pairing students to interact simultaneously to read aloud and discuss their writing, everyone in class can share and respond to the homework in a couple of minutes. In addition to the benefit gained from writing about the homework, students have received the further benefit of speaking and being listened to about it. The time effect of Simultaneous Interaction applies to any writing activity from prewriting to publishing.

Incorporating these four principles in your class activities will insure that you have real, successful cooperative learning happening in your room as opposed to simple group work. These principles are "built-into" the cooperative strategies used throughout the activities.

6. Structures

Structures like RoundRobin and Think-Pair-Share are simple cooperative strategies teachers to use to create learning activities. Structures describe how students interact over the content. There are many structures, each designed to reach different educational objectives.

The activities in this book are based on cooperative structures. Many activities include one cooperative structure, and independent writing. Some activities lead students through a number of cooperative strategies. The procedure for using each cooperative structure is described in each activity The cooperative structure is listed in the Cooperative Learning section of the intro page. A glossary of structures is provided in the back of the book for easy reference.

Multiple Intelligences

The basic premise of multiple intelligences is that people are smart in many ways. Some people

Virginia DeBolt: *Write! Social Studies*
Kagan Publishing • 1 (800) 933-2667

11

are particularly good with words; some people are good with math and logic; some people are especially talented with art and spatial relations; some people are good with their hands and bodies; some people are good with music and rhythm; some people are in tune with others; some people are in tune with themselves; and some people are in tune with nature.

Howard Gardner, the originator or the theory of multiple intelligences, called each one of these ways of being smart an intelligence. He originally identified seven intelligences and has added the eighth, the Naturalist. Gardner's eight intelligences are as follows (see box at right):

1. **Verbal/Linguistic**
2. **Logical/Mathematical**
3. **Visual/Spatial**
4. **Bodily/Kinesthetic**
5. **Musical/Rhythmic**
6. **Interpersonal**
7. **Intrapersonal**
8. **Naturalist**

The implication of the multiple intelligences theory for the classroom is that since students are so diverse, classroom learning should reflect the range of intelligences. Students should be given opportunities to develop their strengths as well as opportunities to develop their weaknesses. See the box below for activities ideas for the multiple intelligences.

Integrating writing and social studies takes naturalist and logical/mathematical content and translates it into a verbal/linguistic form. Teachers can more easily reach and teach linguistic learners. But the activities in this book are much more than solitary writing activities. Being cooperative activities, students work in groups

The 8 Intelligences

Activities for the Multiple Intelligences

Here is a brief list of activities to consider to activate the multiple intelligences.

Verbal/Linguistic
essay, journal, debate, storytelling, portfolios

Logical/Mathematical
out-loud problem solving, puzzles, games, outlines, strategizing

Visual/Spatial
pictorials, flow charts, mindmaps, time lines, models, videotapes, art work

Bodily/Kinesthetic
exhibitions, experiments, models, skits, manipulatives, simulations, role play

Musical/Rhythmic
original songs, dances, rhythmical patterning

Interpersonal
peer review, small group critiques, cooperative learning, leadership

Intrapersonal
reflective journals, goal setting, self-directed projects, self-assessment

Naturalist
observations, logs, categorizing, classifying, experiments

12

Virginia DeBolt: *Write! Social Studies*
Kagan Publishing • 1 (800) 933-2667

and also access and develop their interpersonal intelligence. Additionally, students compose songs, diagram sequences, prioritize alternatives, draw pictures and much more. The multiple intelligences are incorporated throughout the activities. Each activity lists the intelligences used in the Multiple Intelligences section of the intro page.

Higher-Level Thinking

Benjamin Bloom classified different types of thinking skills into a taxonomy, commonly known as Bloom's Taxonomy. His taxonomy of thinking skills is hierarchical. It begins with the lower levels of thinking and moves up to higher-level thinking skills. See Bloom's Taxonomy at left. Higher-level thinking is usually considered thinking skills beyond the knowledge and comprehension levels.

Much emphasis has been placed lately on incorporating higher-level thinking in the subject areas. Writing is a helpful tool in that direction. Writing by its very nature challenges students to move beyond knowledge and comprehension.

Additionally, many of the activities were written with higher-level thinking skills in mind.

Throughout the activities, students apply their knowledge to new situations, use their analytical skills as they delve into issues, pull together different information into a coherent written synthesis, and evaluate the merits of alternatives. The section called Levels of Thinking on the intro page of each activity lists the thinking skills included in the activity corresponding to Bloom's Taxonomy.

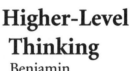

In Summary

Integrating writing and social studies makes social studies come alive and enriches a student's understanding and appreciation of social studies! In this book, you will find a treasure chest of cooperative learning, multiple intelligences, higher-level thinking/ writing activities to integrate writing and social studies!

Bloom's Taxonomy

Higher-Level Thinking

6. Evaluation
5. Synthesis
4. Analysis
3. Application
2. Comprehension
1. Knowledge

Lower-Level Thinking

Virginia DeBolt: *Write! Social Studies*
Kagan Publishing • 1 (800) 933-2667

13

10 Rules for Writers

1. Write.

2. Write.

3. Write Often.

4. Write about anything.

5. Write about everything.

6. Write about what you see.

7. Write about what you learn.

8. Write about what you think.

9. Write about what you read.

10. WRITE!

Virginia DeBolt: *Write! Social Studies*
Kagan Publishing • 1 (800) 933-2667

14

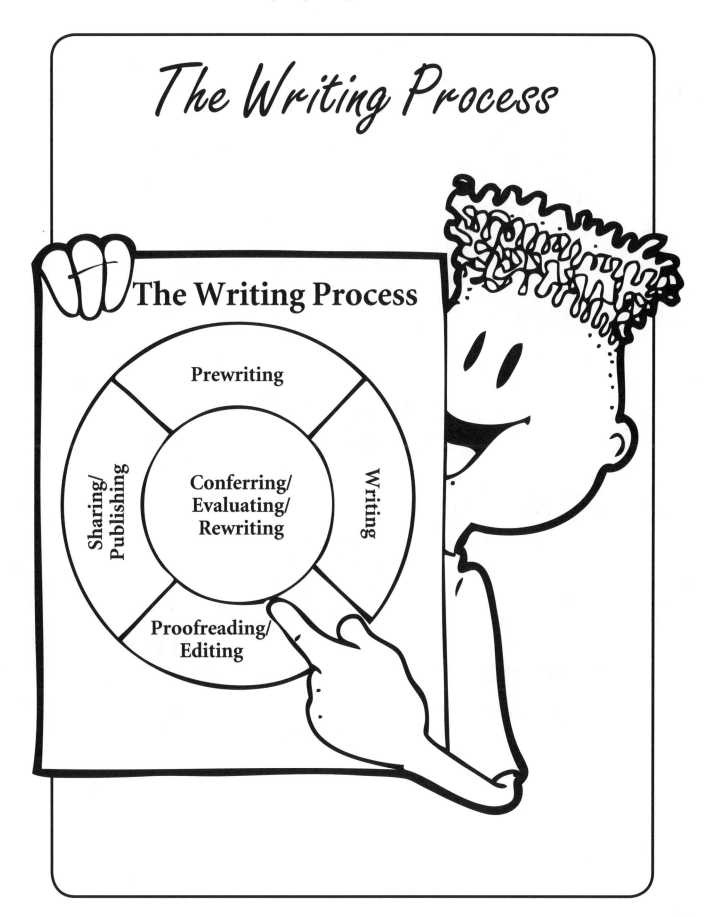

The Writing Process

The Writing Process

- Prewriting
- Writing
- Proofreading/Editing
- Sharing/Publishing
- Conferring/Evaluating/Rewriting

Virginia DeBolt: *Write! Social Studies*
Kagan Publishing • 1 (800) 933-2667

15

Proofreader's Marks

Use these standard marks to show corrections needed in written copy. These symbols are used so that anyone who reads the writing will interpret the corrections in the same way.

⌗
(make a new paragraph)

~~order~~ ❡
(take out)

a̲s she
(capitalize)

some one
(close up space)

∧
(add)

by A̸
(make lowercase)

thier
(reverse letters or words)

⌗
↑
onthe
(insert a space)

soup∧nuts
(add punctuation)

because
~~since~~
(change words)

for her
(move as shown)

⊙
(add a period)

Peer Conference Gambit Cards

Directions: Cut out the cards below. Use these sentence starters when you respond to writing.

I like the part where…

I like the way you used the word _____.

What did you mean when you said…

What happened after…

I liked your beginning because…

I would like to know more about…

I had a clear picture in my mind of the part where…

What would you lose if…

What are you going to do next?

Virginia DeBolt: *Write! Social Studies*
Kagan Publishing • 1 (800) 933-2667

17

Peer Conference Response Form

Author's Name _____

Title _____

Helper's Name _____

Date _____

I like

I want to know more about

One thing you might think about doing

Other

Virginia DeBolt: *Write! Social Studies*
Kagan Publishing • 1 (800) 933-2667

Peer Response	Title _____
	Name _____

Rough Draft

Social Studies Writing Activities

This section of the book consists of thirty-six detailed multiple intelligences, cooperative learning, higher-level thinking activities to assist in teaching and writing about social studies.

The cooperative learning structures used in this section all provide valuable learning experiences, adaptable to any type of content. These structures were selected to lead learners through various stages of thinking and writing about social studies. I hope your experiences using the structures in these social studies activities will open up other ways of applying them in your social studies curriculum.

For the teacher, there are specific ideas for introducing and using the activities and reproducible blackline masters which can be given to the students.

Interspersed through the activities, you will find Journal Topics pages. Journal topics are brief "just write" activities. They can be used in five or ten minutes at the start or close of Social Studies. The use of journals is explained in more depth on pages 6-7.

Virginia DeBolt: *Write! Social Studies*
Kagan Publishing • 1 (800) 933-2667

21

Birthday Events

Some days are filled with exciting local or world news. Some days are rather ho-hum. Regardless, everyday becomes history when a new day rises. One day is very special to students—their birthday. In this activity, students research the events that occurred on the day of their birth. They write a news broadcast for the events and share it with teammates. Learning about their birthday events makes history personally relevant and gives students a sense of personal history.

at-a-glance

Cooperative Structure
• RoundRobin

Level of Thinking
• Comprehension
• Application

Multiple Intelligences
• Verbal/Linguistic
• Interpersonal
• Intrapersonal

IDEA BANK

Ideas for my class . . .	More ideas for my class . . .
Helpful research resources: • Magazine files • Newspaper files • Timelines of history such as "Timelines" by Paul Dickinson • Microfiche	• • • • • • • • •

Independent Write

Have students collect information about world and state events on the day of their birth. Tell students to write a news broadcast, either for television or radio, about events of that day. The broadcast should be written as a script for reading "on the air." Students write their scripts on the reproducible.

RoundRobin

Organize the class into groups of four for the reading of the scripts. Each member of the team reads his or her script in turn until all have read. Within about twenty minutes every student will have read. Walk among the groups during the RoundRobin and choose two or three students to read their scripts to the whole class. Students can then post their scripts, turn them in, or save them in their class three ring binder.

Virginia DeBolt: *Write! Social Studies*
Kagan Publishing • 1 (800) 933-2667

Birthday Events

Name _____ **Date** _____

Directions: Fill in your birthday in the box below. Write the script of a radio or television newscast for the day you were born. Be prepared to share your writing.

My birthday is _____.
                          birthday

Describe the events of your birthday. _____

_____

_____

_____

_____

_____

_____

_____

_____

_____

_____

_____

_____

_____

_____

_____

_____

_____

_____

_____

Virginia DeBolt: *Write! Social Studies*
Kagan Publishing • 1 (800) 933-2667

23

Word Associations

What comes to mind when you hear the word "Democracy?" Words and phrases evoke feelings associated with the topic. In this activity, students write about what they know or how they feel about the topic and share with a partner. This activity can be used as an anticipatory set to assess what students already know or as a culminating review to assess what students have learned.

Ideas for my class . . .	More ideas for my class . . .
What comes to mind when you hear:	•
• Democracy	•
• Nazi	•
• Civil War	•
• Patriot	•
• Civil disobedience	•
• President of the USA	•
• Judicial branch	•
• Refugee	•
• Peace-keeping force	•

IDEA BANK

Think-Write-Pair

Ask students to associate a word (or words) that deals with the learning topic. For example, "What comes to mind when you hear the words "Gold Rush?" Ask students to think without speaking about the associations they have for the topic. Give students fifteen seconds of think time. Then, tell students to write down a quick list of their ideas on a scrap of paper. Have students pair up and share their associations. Students can write down their partner's ideas. Repeat the think-write-pair twice more with a new partner each round. When done, students will have generated and shared lots of ideas related to the topic.

Independent Write

On the reproducible, have students write out their associations.

RoundRobin

Have students take turns sharing their papers with teammates.

Virginia DeBolt: *Write! Social Studies*
Kagan Publishing • 1 (800) 933-2667

Word Associations

Directions: Fill in the topic in the box below. Write about what comes to mind when you hear the word. Be prepared to share your paper.

What comes to mind when you hear _____ .
topic

Write what comes to mind when you hear the topic. _____

_____

_____

_____

_____

_____

_____

_____

_____

_____

_____

_____

_____

_____

_____

_____

_____

_____

_____

_____

_____

Virginia DeBolt: *Write! Social Studies*
Kagan Publishing • 1 (800) 933-2667

25

Social Studies Skit

Make social studies come alive through skits. In this activity, students work in teams to write and rehearse a skit. Teams perform their skit for the class. Skits create experiential learning for students, activate the bodily/kinesthetic intelligence and are a lot of fun to do.

ACTIVITY 3

at-a-glance

Cooperative Structures

• Team Project
• Teams Present
• RoundRobin

Level of Thinking

• Knowledge
• Analysis
• Synthesis

Multiple Intelligences

• Verbal/Linguistic
• Visual/Spatial
• Bodily/Kinesthetic
• Interpersonal

Ideas for my class . . .	More ideas for my class . . .
Write and perform a skit on: • Prohibition • American Revolution • Pilgrims landing on Plymouth Rock • Attack on Pearl Harbor • Custer's Last Stand • Cuban Missile Crisis • Gold Rush	• • • • • • • •

IDEA BANK

Team Project

Assign the class a skit relating to the topic of study. For example, the topic may be the Prohibition. (See the Idea Bank for more ideas.) Tell students that they must write a skit that captures the essence of the topic, rehearse their skit and perform it for the class. Give students a time limit and tell them that every student must have an active role in the skit.

In teams, students discuss how they want to perform the topic. for example, one team may decide to perform the gangster aspect of the Prohibition. Another team may decide to depict a speakeasy scene. Another team may show a bootlegging operation. A fourth team might be law enforcement officers. Each team will have their own interpretation of the event or time period and each skit should be unique. Teams write the dialogue for their skit on paper so students can rehearse their skit. Teams can turn in their skits for feedback. Writing and preparing the skits may be an on-going project.

Teams Present

When teams have rehearsed their skits and memorized their lines

Virginia DeBolt: *Write! Social Studies*
Kagan Publishing • 1 (800) 933-2667

they take turns performing
their skit for the class.

Independent Write

After all teams have performed
their skit, students can write
a paper on the reproducible
about what they learned about
the topic.

RoundRobin

In teams, students take turns
reading their skit reflection to
teammates.

Virginia DeBolt: *Write! Social Studies*
Kagan Publishing • 1 (800) 933-2667

27

Social Studies Skit

Name _____ **Date** _____

Directions: Fill in the topic of the skit in the box below. Write about what you saw, what you liked, and what you learned from the skits. Be prepared to share your reflections with teammates.

My reflections on _____ .
                                          skit topic

_____

_____

_____

_____

_____

_____

_____

_____

_____

_____

_____

_____

_____

_____

_____

_____

_____

_____

_____

_____

_____

Virginia DeBolt: *Write! Social Studies*
Kagan Publishing • 1 (800) 933-2667

Journal Topics

- What law does our town need?

- You are an explorer looking for a perfect place to build a city. Describe the place.

- If you went to Jupiter and set up a new government, what would it be like?

- Give the top five reasons why a woman would be a good president. (Even if you don't believe it!)

Virginia DeBolt: *Write! Social Studies*
Kagan Publishing • 1 (800) 933-2667

29

Speaking with Roles

Make historical characters come alive for your class. In this activity, students are each assigned a historical figure. Students research their historical figures in pairs, write a speech from the character's perspective and share their speeches with teammates. Students, in role, are interviewed by their teammates.

ACTIVITY

4

at-a-glance

Cooperative Structures

• Jigsaw
• RoundRobin
• Team Interview

Level of Thinking

• Knowledge
• Comprehension
• Application
• Synthesis

Multiple Intelligences

• Verbal/Linguistic
• Visual/Spatial
• Bodily/Kinesthetic
• Interpersonal

Ideas for my class . . .	*More ideas for my class . . .*	I D E A B A N K
• Use this activity with any historical figures from your curriculum.	• • • • • • • • • •	

Jigsaw

Select four historical characters from the unit of study or topic. For example, if studying presidents, you may pick Lincoln, Truman, Washington, Kennedy. Write the figure's name on the chalkboard along with a research question about the figure: "Lincoln: What would Lincoln have said about the first battle of the Civil War? Truman: What would Truman have said after the Japanese surrender in World War II? Assign each student on the team a different figure. Have all the Lincolns meet in one corner of the class, the Washingtons in another and so on. In their character-alike corners, students pair up to research their figure.

Independent Write

After a predetermined amount of time, tell students to write a speech about the topic from the point of view of their historical person.

Virginia DeBolt: *Write! Social Studies*
Kagan Publishing • 1 (800) 933-2667

RoundRobin

Have students form groups of four in their character-alike corners and take turns reading their speeches. After each student reads, teammates offer ideas for improvement.

Independent Write

Students work independently to rewrite their speeches based on the feedback they received.

Team Interview

Students reunite with their original teammates so that each person has a different historical character. Student One stands and reads his or her speech to teammates. When done, teammates ask him or her questions about the character which he or she answers in role.

Student Two goes next. This continues until all students have shared their speech and answered questions in role. To spice up the team interview, encourage students to "get into" role with costumes and props.

Virginia DeBolt: *Write! Social Studies*
Kagan Publishing • 1 (800) 933-2667

31

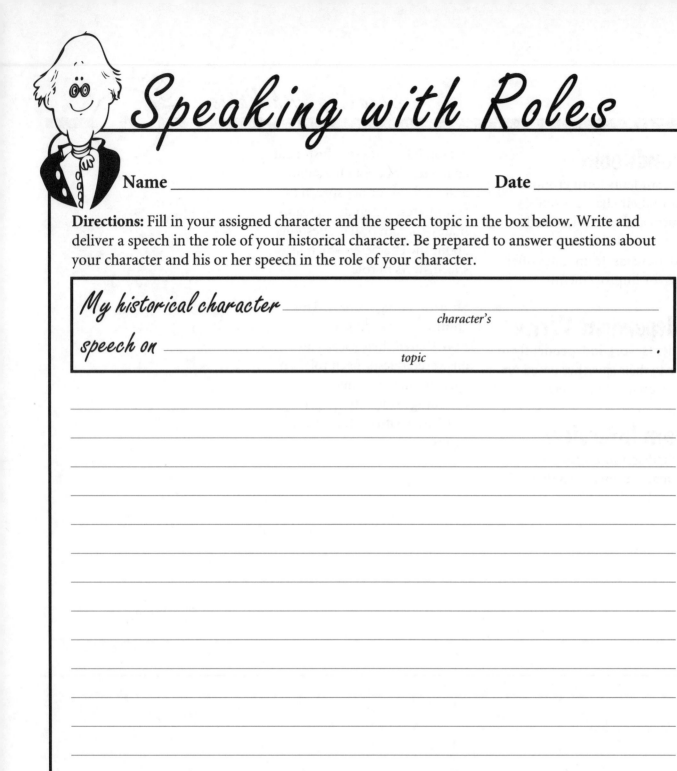

Speaking with Roles

Name _____ **Date** _____

Directions: Fill in your assigned character and the speech topic in the box below. Write and deliver a speech in the role of your historical character. Be prepared to answer questions about your character and his or her speech in the role of your character.

My historical character _____
                                                                      character's
speech on _____ .
                                    topic

_____
_____
_____
_____
_____
_____
_____
_____
_____
_____
_____
_____
_____
_____
_____
_____
_____
_____
_____
_____
_____
_____

Virginia DeBolt: *Write! Social Studies*
Kagan Publishing • 1 (800) 933-2667

Journal Topics

- Why do you think the oldest part of town is near the railroad tracks?

- Rewrite the Bill of Rights as a rap.

- What is the most important thing to spend money to buy?

- What are three things you could do to help the people of your town?

Virginia DeBolt: *Write! Social Studies*
Kagan Publishing • 1 (800) 933-2667

33

Historical Correspondence

What might Abraham Lincoln and Sojourner Truth have written to each other? Benito Mussolini and Franklin Delano Roosevelt? Dwight Eisenhower and Anne Frank? Or characters from different times such as O. J. Simpson and Clarence Darrow? In this activity, students write the correspondence between the historical figures.

Materials Needed

- Crayons or markers, envelopes, and scissors.
- Nick Bantock books as examples of correspondence

Cooperative Structures

- Pair Project
- RoundRobin

Level of Thinking

- Analysis
- Synthesis

Multiple Intelligences

- Verbal/Linguistic
- Logical/Mathematical
- Visual/Spatial
- Interpersonal

Ideas for my class . . .	More ideas for my class . . .
Write the correspondence of: • Kennedy and Castro • Churchill and Hitler • Geronimo and Cleveland • Reagan and Gorbachev • Harriet Beetcher Stowe and Lincoln • Pocohantas and John Smith	• • • • • • • • •

IDEA BANK

Pair Project

Announce two historical figures to the class relating to the topic of study. For example, if studying the Civil War, perhaps you would select Robert E. Lee and Ulysses S. Grant. Have pairs research the two characters, the time they lived in, and what they might have said to each other in correspondence.

Independent Write

Students independently write their first draft of a correspon-

dence between the historical figures. They can select either figure to begin the correspondence. The correspondence should include facts about the events and time and be true to the character's personality.

RoundRobin

Have students get back into teams of four to share their correspondence. Each teammate reads his or her letters to teammates. When done, teammates offer suggestions

Virginia DeBolt: *Write! Social Studies*
Kagan Publishing • 1 (800) 933-2667

for improvement. The forms at the end of Part I may be helpful for peer conferences.

Independent Write

Students rewrite a final draft of their correspondence based on feedback from their teammates. Encourage students to make the final drafts look like the actual correspondence between the two characters. For example, Grant and Lee's correspondence might have been on war-tattered post-cards or highly formal parchment with calligraphy. When done, students can post their correspondence somewhere in the class to share with classmates or can exchange their correspondences.

Virginia DeBolt: *Write! Social Studies*
Kagan Publishing • 1 (800) 933-2667

35

Historical Correspondence

Name _____ **Date** _____

Directions: Create a correspondence between two historical characters. Be true to the times and personalities of the characters.

Date _____

Dear _____ ,

_____

_____

_____

_____

_____

_____

Sincerely,

_____

Date _____

Dear _____ ,

_____

_____

_____

_____

_____

_____

Sincerely,

_____

Virginia DeBolt: *Write! Social Studies*
Kagan Publishing • 1 (800) 933-2667

Journal Topics

- Write about yesterday's homework.

- Write three questions about the reading assignment.

- Write a one sentence summary of each section of the chapter.

- What was the most important thing you learned in class today?

Virginia DeBolt: *Write! Social Studies*
Kagan Publishing • 1 (800) 933-2667

37

Interview History's Celebrities

If Benjamin Franklin was alive today, what would you ask him? What would you ask Susan B. Anthony? In this activity, students brainstorm interview questions to ask historical figures then write a fictitious interview with the character and share it with teammates.

ACTIVITY 6

at-a-glance

Cooperative Structures

• ThinkPad Brainstorming
• RoundRobin

Level of Thinking

• Application
• Synthesis

Multiple Intelligences

• Verbal/Linguistic
• Interpersonal

Ideas for my class . . .	More ideas for my class . . .
Interview: • People in the current chapter • People in the daily news • Local, state and national officials	• • • • • • • • •

IDEA BANK

ThinkPad Brainstorming

Announce a historical character to the class. For example, if studying the Prohibition, Al Capone may be an interesting person to interview. In teams, students come up with questions to ask their character, writing each one on a separate slip of paper and placing it in the middle of the table or desks for teammates to see. After a few minutes of brainstorming ideas, students take turns reading the questions they generated for the character.

Independent Write

Students select their favorite interview questions for the character. They write a fictitious interview with their character on the reproducible.

RoundRobin

Students take turns reading their interviews to teammates.

Virginia DeBolt: *Write! Social Studies*
Kagan Publishing • 1 (800) 933-2667

Interview History's Celebrities

Name _____ Date _____

Directions: Fill in the historical character in the box below. Write an imaginary interview with this historical character.

My interview with _____ .
                              historical character

Write an interview with this character. _____

_____

_____

_____

_____

_____

_____

_____

_____

_____

_____

_____

_____

_____

_____

_____

_____

_____

_____

_____

Social Studies Jeopardy

Jeopardy is a fun way to learn or review the content of the chapter or unit. In this activity, students write questions and answers relating to the topic. In teams, students quiz each other by providing the answer and asking for the appropriate question.

Cooperative Structure

• RoundRobin

Level of Thinking

• Knowledge
• Comprehension
• Application

Multiple Intelligences

• Verbal/Linguistic
• Logical/Mathematical
• Visual/Spatial
• Interpersonal
• Naturalist

Ideas for my class . . .	More ideas for my class . . .
Play Jeopardy with: • Vocabulary words • Events • Dates • People in history • Geographic information • Map skills	• • • • • • • • • •

IDEA BANK

Independent Write

Students use their texts or notes to write as many review questions and answers as they can. It is essential that the answer be framed in a way that there is only one correct question. They may be written on the reproducible.

RoundRobin

After students have a number of review questions and answers, students read an answer to the team. For example, a president answer may be: "He was the first President to reach office without being elected to it." The first teammate to raise his or her hand gets to provide the question, "Who is Gerald Ford?"

Students can play for points. A less competitive alternative is to have the teammate to the left get the first opportunity to provide the question to the answer. This can also be done on flashcards to send problems to other teams to answer. Jeopardy can also be played as a class, with teams competing against each other.

Virginia DeBolt: *Write! Social Studies*
Kagan Publishing • 1 (800) 933-2667

Social Studies Jeopardy

Name _____ **Date** _____

Directions: Fill in the review topic in the box below. Write as many review questions and answers as you can. Read your answer and see if your teammates can provide the right question.

_____ Jeopardy
topic

A _____

Q _____

A _____

Q _____

A _____

Q _____

A _____

Q _____

A _____

Q _____

Virginia DeBolt: *Write! Social Studies*
Kagan Publishing • 1 (800) 933-2667

41

Quote and Comment

Write a quotation on the board relating to the topic of study, then have students discuss the quotation in pairs. Students write their analysis or evaluation of the quote and share their writing with teammates. This is a great way to get students thinking about the topic, and can be done daily at the beginning or end of class.

ACTIVITY 8

at-a-glance

Cooperative Structures

• Think-Pair-Share
• RoundRobin

Level of Thinking

• Analysis

Multiple Intelligences

• Verbal/Linguistic
• Interpersonal

Ideas for my class . . .	More ideas for my class . . .
Use quotes from: • The writings of people in your current chapter • Famous speeches • Textbook • Philosophies • Famous people	• • • • • • • • •

IDEA BANK

Think-Pair-Share

Write the quotation on the board. (Try one of the sample quotes on the following page.) Before students do any writing, lead them through several rounds of Think-Pair-Share. Instruct students to read the quotation and think about its meaning. Allow fifteen to thirty seconds of think time. Students pair to discuss what they think the quotation means. Select a pair or two share with the class. Then instruct the students to think about issues relevant to the quote. Think time is again followed by pair work and sharing. Repeat the steps, directing students to think about the time in which the speaker lived. Finally, the teacher instructs the students to think about what importance the quote has for people today. Each pairing can be done with a new partner. Pick different students to share with the class.

Independent Write

Have students write their comments about the quotation on the reproducible.

RoundRobin

Students take turns sharing their writing with teammates.

42

Virginia DeBolt: *Write! Social Studies*
Kagan Publishing • 1 (800) 933-2667

Sample Quotations

"Victory at all costs, victory in spite of all terror, victory however long and hard the road may be; for without victory there is no survival."
—Winston Churchill

"The first requisite of a good citizen in this Republic of ours is that he shall be able and willing to pull his weight."
—Theodore Roosevelt

"I heartily accept the motto, 'That government is best which governs least'; and I should like to see it acted up to more rapidly and systematically. Carried out, it finally amounts to this, which I also believe—'That government is best which governs not at all.'"
—Henry David Thoreau

"And so, my fellow Americans: ask not what your country can do for you—ask what you can do for your country. My fellow citizens of the world: ask not what America will do for you, but what together we can do for the freedom of man."
—John Fitzgerald Kennedy

Virginia DeBolt: *Write! Social Studies*
Kagan Publishing • 1 (800) 933-2667

43

Quote and Comment

Name _____ **Date** _____

Directions: Copy the quotation from the board. Write for several minutes about what you think the quote means, what it refers to, what it teaches us about the time in which the speaker lived, and what relevance it has for people today.

Quotation: _____

_____

_____

_____

My analysis: _____

_____

_____

_____

_____

_____

_____

_____

_____

_____

_____

_____

_____

_____

_____

_____

_____

_____

Virginia DeBolt: *Write! Social Studies*
Kagan Publishing • 1 (800) 933-2667

Journal Topics

- Write riddles for which the answer is a vocabulary

- Write about a question you missed on the homework assignment.

- Apply today's lesson to politics.

- Apply today's lesson to economics.

Virginia DeBolt: *Write! Social Studies*
Kagan Publishing • 1 (800) 933-2667

45

Earth's Answers

In one sense, geography is the history of political struggle. Yet under the boundaries and divisions of nations and states lies the earth itself. Suppose the earth could speak—what would it say? In this activity, students ask the earth about landforms, features, ecological health, the cycles of nature, or human use of its resources.

Cooperative Structures

- Jigsaw Problem Solving
- RoundRobin
- Teams Present

Level of Thinking

- Synthesis

Multiple Intelligences

- Verbal/Linguistic
- Logical/Mathematical
- Visual/Spatial
- Bodily/Kinesthetic
- Musical/Rhythmic
- Interpersonal
- Naturalist

Ideas for my class . . .	More ideas for my class . . .
Ask the earth about: • Volcanos, glaciers, canyons, earthquakes and other earth shaping features.	• • • • • • • • • •

I D E A   B A N K

Jigsaw Problem Solving

Come up with four research questions relating to the topic of study. For example, if studying mountains the four questions might be:

1. How were mountains formed?
2. How do mountains affect surrounding land?
3. What are the ecological characteristics of mountains?
4. What are some famous mountains, and why are they famous?

Assign each student on the team one of the four questions. Students with the same questions meet in one of the four corners of the classroom. Students pair up with another student with the same question and work together to answer the question.

Independent Write

Students independently write their answer to the question, framing it as if it was the Earth's answer to their question.

RoundRobin

Students reunite with their original team and share the Earth's answer to their questions.

Teams Present

Teams can synthesize their independent writing into a coherent "Conversation with the earth." The conversation can be turned into a collage, skit, or song and presented to another team or to the whole class.

Virginia DeBolt: *Write! Social Studies*
Kagan Publishing • 1 (800) 933-2667

46

Earth's Answers

Name _____ **Date** _____

Directions: Fill in your question for Earth in the box below. Write Earth's answer to your question. Be prepared to share Earth's answer with teammates.

My question for Earth _____ .

question

Earth's answer _____

_____

_____

_____

_____

_____

_____

_____

_____

_____

_____

_____

_____

_____

_____

_____

_____

_____

Virginia DeBolt: *Write! Social Studies*
Kagan Publishing • 1 (800) 933-2667

47

Compare & Contrast

Social Studies is loaded with great topics to compare and contrast. Students can compare and contrast historical events, historical figures, parties, laws and much more. By comparing and contrasting, students learn about the details of topics being studied and develop strong analytical skills. In this activity, students brainstorm how two things are similar and different and write compare and contrast essays on the topic.

Cooperative Structures

• ThinkPad Brainstorming
• Teams Present
• RoundRobin

Level of Thinking

• Analysis
• Synthesis

Multiple Intelligences

• Verbal/Linguistic
• Visual/Spatial
• Logical/Mathematical
• Interpersonal

Ideas for my class . . .	More ideas for my class . . .
Compare and Contrast:	•
• Senator/House of Representatives	•
• China/Japan	•
• Lincoln/Washington	•
• World War I/WW II	•
• 1920's/1930's	•
• Democrats/Republicans	•
• Articles of Confederation/ Constitution	•

IDEA BANK

ThinkPad Brainstorming

Announce the topics to compare and contrast. For example, if studying government, student may compare and contrast Republicans and Democrats. On a large sheet of paper, have each team draw a large Venn dia-gram and label it with the topics to compare and contrast. (See graphic.) Students brainstorm things that they have in common and ways they differ, writing each idea on a separate thinkpad and placing it in the Venn diagram.

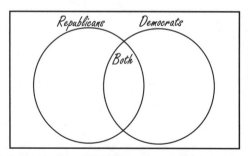

Teams Present

Teams can share their completed Venn diagrams with one other team or several other teams.

Independent Write

After students have generated lots of ideas and have seen the ideas of others, they each write their own

Virginia DeBolt: *Write! Social Studies*
Kagan Publishing • 1 (800) 933-2667

compare and contrast papers. The ideas in the section of the Venn where the two circles intersect can be the basis for the comparisons and the ideas that are distinct to the two parties can be the basis of the contrasts.

RoundRobin
Students take turns reading their compare and contrast essays to teammates.

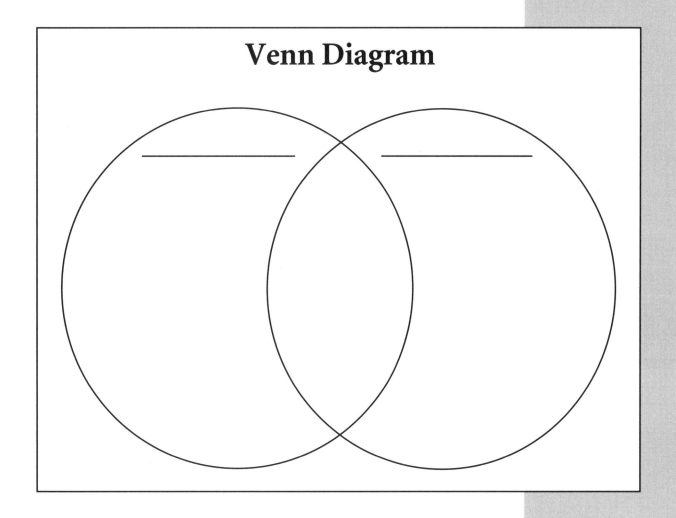

Venn Diagram

_____   _____

Virginia DeBolt: *Write! Social Studies*
Kagan Publishing • 1 (800) 933-2667

49

Compare & Contrast

Name _____ **Period** _____ **Date** _____

Directions: Fill in the topics to compare and contrast in the box below. Write a paper comparing and contrasting the two topics.

Compare and contrast _____ and _____ .

Compare and contrast the two topics. _____

_____

_____

_____

_____

_____

_____

_____

_____

_____

_____

_____

_____

_____

_____

_____

_____

_____

_____

Virginia DeBolt: *Write! Social Studies*
Kagan Publishing • 1 (800) 933-2667

Journal Topics

- Pick a vocabulary word. How many other words can you make out of its letters?

- Think of five research projects that deal with today's chapter. Which would be the most interesting?

- Should people try to save endangered species? Why or why not?

- How does a "good citizen" behave?

Virginia DeBolt: *Write! Social Studies*
Kagan Publishing • 1 (800) 933-2667

51

Social Studies Songs

Do you seem to remember all the lyrics to songs you haven't even heard in years? Putting the curriculum to music not only makes learning fun, but it also helps with mastery of concepts and recall, especially for your musically inclined students. In this activity, pairs work together to create a social studies song. They sing their song to the class as a duet.

ACTIVITY 11

at-a-glance

Cooperative Structures

• Think-Pair-Share
• Pair Project
• Pairs Present

Level of Thinking

• Synthesis
• Evaluation

Multiple Intelligences

• Verbal/Linguistic
• Logical/Mathematical
• Musical/Rhythmic
• Interpersonal

Ideas for my class . . .	More ideas for my class . . .
Write a song about:	•
• President	•
• Passing a law	•
• Civil rights activist	•
• Women in history	•
• Democracy	•
• The Bill of Rights	•
• Revolution	•
• Slavery	•
	•

IDEA BANK

Think-Pair-Share

Songs are much easier for students to write if they are written to a familiar tune. Have students generate familiar tunes: "What are some familiar tunes that everyone knows?" Give students some think time, then have students pair with a partner to list their ideas. Pick several students to share their ideas with the class. Record their tune ideas on the chalkboard. For example, students may come up with: Jingle Bells, When the Saints Go Marching In, My Bonnie Lies Over the Ocean, Old MacDonald, Mary Had Little Lamb, Three Blind Mice, Rudolph the Red-Nose Reindeer. Students may also come up with popular songs which are a little more "cool."

Pair Project

When students have a list of song ideas, have them pair up. Assign the class a topic about which to write a social studies song. (See the ideas in the Idea Bank above.)

52

Virginia DeBolt: *Write! Social Studies*
Kagan Publishing • 1 (800) 933-2667

Pairs select a tune, then work together to write the lyrics to their song. The song should contain facts about the topic. Use Bunker Hill below as an example.

Pairs Present

Pairs take turns singing their social studies song to the class. A quicker sharing alternative is to have pairs share with another pair, or do several rounds of sharing.

Sample Social Studies Song

Bunker Hill
(Sung to the tune of Yankee Doodle)

Bunker Hill, the first big battle
Of the Revolution
Patriots would fight for rights
And fight to resolution!
Revolution underway
Thoughts of freedom sowing
Patriots attacking when
The "whites of eyes" were showing!

Major Prescott went to battle
On a hill near Boston
The Redcoats lost a lot of men
The battle really cost'em!
Redcoats tried to take the hill
Patriots kept shooting
Redcoats ran away two times
And found themselves regrouping!

Bunker Hill, the first big battle
Of the Revolution
Patriots would fight for rights
And fight to resolution!
Revolution underway
Thoughts of freedom sowing
Patriots attacking when
The "whites of eyes" were showing!

The Patriots were feeling good
Because they didn't cower
But soon they knew their fight was through
When they ran out of powder
Redcoats charged the hill again
Patriots were fleeing
They were forced to leave the hill
Or stay and take a beating!!

Bunker Hill, the first big battle
Of the Revolution
Patriots would fight for rights
And fight to resolution!
Revolution underway
Thoughts of freedom sowing
Patriots attacking when
The "whites of eyes" were showing!

From: **Lyrical Lessons by**
Clint Klose & Larry Wolfe,
Kagan Cooperative Learning.

Virginia DeBolt: *Write! Social Studies*
Kagan Publishing • 1 (800) 933-2667

53

Social Studies Songs

Name _____ **Date** _____

Directions: Fill in the topic and tune of your social studies song in the box below. Write your song to a familiar tune. Don't forget to include all relevant facts about your topic. Be prepared to share your song with the class.

Our Social Studies song on _____ .
                                          topic
To the tune of _____ .
                                tune

_____

_____

_____

_____

_____

_____

_____

_____

_____

_____

_____

_____

_____

_____

_____

_____

_____

_____

_____

Virginia DeBolt: *Write! Social Studies*
Kagan Publishing • 1 (800) 933-2667

Journal Topics

- Write a letter to a parent about today's class.

- Write a poem using the vocabulary words.

- How could you express today's lesson with a map?

- Write five questions you would like to ask a historical figure.

Virginia DeBolt: *Write! Social Studies*
Kagan Publishing • 1 (800) 933-2667

55

The Me Map

In this activity, students mark on a map of the world where they and their ancestors came from. Students write about their cultural background and share it with teammates. This activity promotes appreciation of cultural diversity, geography knowledge and makes the content more personally relevant.

Cooperative Structure

• Team Interview

Level of Thinking

• Knowledge
• Comprehension
• Application

Multiple Intelligences

• Verbal/Linguistic
• Visual/Spatial
• Interpersonal
• Intrapersonal

Ideas for my class . . .	More ideas for my class . . .
Other multicultural ideas: • Have students write about holidays and celebrities from around the world • Have students compare cultures • Have students create flags and write about the country on the back.	• • • • • • • • •

IDEA BANK

Independent Write

On the Me Map reproducible, students mark on the world map where they come from, where their parents came from, where their grandparents came from, and where their great grandparents came from. It may be helpful to have students fill out their maps at home with their parents. Students write a description of their cultural and geographical roots. This assignment can easily be a report. Encourage students to bring in cultural items such as money, clothing, pictures, stamps to share with teammates or with the class.

Team Interview

In their teams, students take turns showing teammates their filled-in maps and reading their descriptions of their ancestry. After each student shares, he or she is interviewed by teammates for a minute or two. Teammates ask questions like: "When did you come to America? Do you still have relatives outside of the U.S.? Do you observe any cultural traditions from another country?"

Extension Activity

Make a "Where We Come From" bulletin board indicating the cultural and geographical roots of each student in the class. The bulletin board can be a large map or the world with push pins holding up name cards and country or state names for each student.

56

Virginia DeBolt: *Write! Social Studies*
Kagan Publishing • 1 (800) 933-2667

The Me Map

Name _____ **Date** _____

Directions: In the blanks below, write in the country you and your ancestors came from. Draw a line from each ancestor to the world map indicating where each person came from. On the back of this paper, or on a separate sheet, write about your geographical and cultural background, including that of your ancestors.

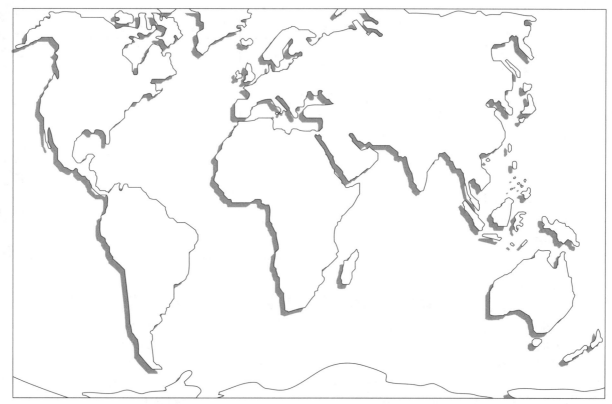

• Me _____

• Mom _____   • Dad _____

• Grandma _____   • Grandma _____

• Grandpa _____   • Grandpa _____

• Great Grandma _____   • Great Grandma _____

• Great Grandpa _____   • Great Grandpa _____

Virginia DeBolt: *Write! Social Studies*
Kagan Publishing • 1 (800) 933-2667

57

Team Travelers

Some students have been to exotic corners of the world; some have never left the state. In this activity, students write about and share their travels. This a fun way to broaden students' global awareness and bring students' personal experiences into learning.

at-a-glance

Cooperative Structures

• RoundRobin
• Team Project
• Teams Present

Level of Thinking

• Knowledge
• Comprehension
• Application
• Analysis
• Evaluation

Multiple Intelligences

• Verbal/Linguistic
• Visual/Spatial
• Interpersonal
• Intrapersonal

Ideas for my class...	More ideas for my class...
Describe places you've been: • In our neighborhood • In our state • In the U.S. • In the world	• • • • • • • • • •

IDEA BANK

Independent Write

Ask students to think of all the places they've ever been. Have them make a list on a scrap of paper. When students each have a list of places they've lived or visited, have them pick their three most interesting places and write a description of each on the reproducible.

RoundRobin

In teams, students take turns sharing the places they've been with teammates.

Team Project

After all teammates have shared where they've been, the team can make a team poster of places they've visited. Another idea is to have the team make a brochure for one of the places a teammate has been.

Teams Present

Teams can share their posters or brochures with another team or pass them in the room to share with classmates.

Virginia DeBolt: *Write! Social Studies*
Kagan Publishing • 1 (800) 933-2667

Team Travelers

Name _____ **Date** _____

Directions: Fill in the information for the three most interesting places you've been. Include the name of the place, the country or state, how old you were, how you got there, how long you stayed and your general comments about the location. Be prepared to share your travels with teammates.

Place _____ Age _____
Travel method _____ Duration _____
Comments _____
_____
_____
_____

Place _____ Age _____
Travel method _____ Duration _____
Comments _____
_____
_____
_____

Place _____ Age _____
Travel method _____ Duration _____
Comments _____
_____
_____
_____

Virginia DeBolt: *Write! Social Studies*
Kagan Publishing • 1 (800) 933-2667

59

Map Interpretation

Astute map readers can induce generalities about an area when presented with specifics on a map. For example, seeing little ears of corn on the map tells you more than corn grows there. It speaks volumes about the landforms, water supplies, soil condition, life styles, population. In this activity, students develop their map reading skills by reaching conclusions based on specifics.

Ideas for my class . . .	More ideas for my class . . .
Interpret:	•
• Resources maps	•
• Population maps	•
• Product maps	•
• Rainfall maps	•
• Elevation maps	•
• Climate maps	•
• Picture maps	•
	•

IDEA BANK

Independent Write

Assign the class a map to interpret. Have students use the reproducible to write what they see on the map and what it tells them about the area. For example, under "What I see," students may write, "The Rocky Mountains are colored in beige and yellow." Under "What it tells me," students may write, "The Rocky Mountains contain the greatest expanse of high elevation mountains in the U.S., reaching over 10,000 in elevation with the highest concentration in central Colorado."

RoundRobin

In teams, students take turns sharing their map interpretations with teammates.

Team Discussion

The team discusses their map interpretations. Teammates help each students pick his or her most insightful map interpretation.

Stand and Share

All students stand beside their desks. Select one student to share his or her most insightful map interpretation with the class. He or she sits down as do all other students in the room who had essentially the same information to share. Keep selecting students to share until all students are seated.

60

Virginia DeBolt: *Write! Social Studies*
Kagan Publishing • 1 (800) 933-2667

Map Interpretation

Name _____ **Date** _____

Directions: Fill in the name or type of map you are interpreting in the box below. Write what you see on the map and what it tells you about the area.

My interpretation of _____ .
                                                    map

What I see _____
What it tells me _____
_____

What I see _____
What it tells me _____
_____

What I see _____
What it tells me _____
_____

What I see _____
What it tells me _____
_____

What I see _____
What it tells me _____
_____

Virginia DeBolt: *Write! Social Studies*
Kagan Publishing • 1 (800) 933-2667

61

Cause and Effect

What caused the Great Depression? How about World War II? What caused the westward movement? In this activity, students explore the various causes of historical events.

at-a-glance

Cooperative Structure

• RoundTable

Level of Thinking

• Analysis
• Synthesis
• Evaluation

Multiple Intelligences

• Verbal/Linguistic
• Logical/Mathematical
• Interpersonal

Ideas for my class . . .	More ideas for my class . . .
What is the cause of:	•
• Civil War	•
• Abolition	•
• Gold Rush	•
• Vietnam War	•
• Revolutionary War	•
• Prohibition	•
• Women's suffrage	•
	•
	•

IDEA BANK

RoundTable

Announce one historical event relating to the topic of study. For example, the event may be the Revolutionary War: "What caused the Revolutionary War?" In teams, Student One writes one cause of the revolution on a sheet of paper. He or she may write "Taxes." They continue generating causes until they've exhausted the topic. If a teammate can not think of a cause, he or she may ask teammates for help. Then, they work together to recall or investigate as much information they can about each cause.

Independent Write

Students work independently to write an essay on the causes of the historical event. They can use their team ideas to help them write their essay.

Virginia DeBolt: *Write! Social Studies*
Kagan Publishing • 1 (800) 933-2667

Cause and Effect

Name _____ Date _____

Directions: Fill in the historical event in the box below. Write what caused this event.

What is the cause of _____ ?
                                            event

Describe the causes of the event. _____

_____

_____

_____

_____

_____

_____

_____

_____

_____

_____

_____

_____

_____

_____

_____

_____

_____

_____

_____

Virginia DeBolt: *Write! Social Studies*
Kagan Publishing • 1 (800) 933-2667

63

Analyze the Difference

Analyzing the difference is contrasting without comparing. A Venn diagram is often used for comparing and contrasting. A graphic organizer is also helpful for analyzing the difference, but in this case, the circles of the Venn do not intersect, as students are not exploring similarities. In this activity, students analyze the difference in key social studies concepts.

ACTIVITY
16

at-a-glance

Cooperative Structure

• Think-Write-
  Pair-Square

Level of Thinking

• Analysis

Multiple Intelligences

• Verbal/Linguistic
• Visual/Spatial
• Interpersonal

Ideas for my class . . .	More ideas for my class . . .
Analyze the difference between: • Civil War/Revolution • Election of senators/ appointment of Supreme Court justices • Gulf/bay • Legal right/civic duty • Contributions/ bribery • Republican/Democrat	• • • • • • • • •

IDEA BANK

Think-Write-Pair-Square

Give students two topics to analyze the difference. For example, "What are the differences between Martin Luther King Jr. and Malcolm X?" On a separate sheet of paper, have student draw two non-intersecting circles and label them with the topics assigned. See graphic.

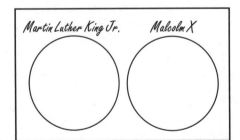

Give students time to think, then have them list as many differences as they can in the graphic organizer. Have students pair up and compare their differences. Students can record any of their partner's ideas in their graphic organizer. Pairs join another pair to form a team of four. The pairs compare and discuss their differences. Again, encourage students to record ideas in their graphic organizer.

Independent Write

Using the ideas they generated with teammates, students write their own papers analyzing the difference between the two topics on the reproducible.

64

Virginia DeBolt: *Write! Social Studies*
Kagan Publishing • 1 (800) 933-2667

Analyze the Difference

Directions: Fill in the topics to analyze the differences in the box below. Write a paper analyzing the difference.

What are the differences between _____ topic 1

and _____ ?
topic 2

Describe the differences. _____

_____

_____

_____

_____

_____

_____

_____

_____

_____

_____

_____

_____

_____

_____

_____

_____

_____

_____

_____

Virginia DeBolt: *Write! Social Studies*
Kagan Publishing • 1 (800) 933-2667

65

Commonalities

What do the Vietnam War and the Korean War have in common? What do Martin Luther King Jr. and Gandhi have in common? In this activity, students analyze historical events or characters for their commonalities.

ACTIVITY
17

at-a-glance

Cooperative Structures

• RallyTable
• Pair Discussion
• RoundRobin

Level of Thinking

• Analysis
• Synthesis

Multiple Intelligences

• Verbal/Linguistic
• Logical/Mathematical
• Interpersonal

Ideas for my class . . .	More ideas for my class . . .
What are the commonalities between: • Articles of Confederation/ Constitution • Socialism/communism • United States/France • Plateau/mountain • Grant/Washington • Capitalism/Puritanism	• • • • • • • • • •

IDEA BANK

RallyTable

Announce the topic to the class. For example, "What do the Mayans and the Aztecs have in common?" On a sheet of paper, have pairs draw two large intersecting circles and label them. (See graphic.) Partners take turns recording the commonalities.

Pair Discussion

When students have a list of ideas of what the topics have in common they discuss how they would organize an essay about the commonalities using the ideas they generated. They can work together in creating an outline for an essay.

Independent Write

On the reproducible, students independently write about the commonalities.

RoundRobin

Student take turns sharing their essay on commonalities with teammates.

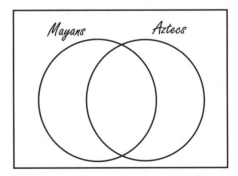

Virginia DeBolt: *Write! Social Studies*
Kagan Publishing • 1 (800) 933-2667

66

Commonalities

Name _____ **Date** _____

Directions: Fill in the topics in the box below. Write an essay describing what the two topics have in common.

What do _____ *and* _____
have in common?　　　　topic 1　　　　　　　　　　　topic 2

Describe the commonalities. _____

_____

_____

_____

_____

_____

_____

_____

_____

_____

_____

_____

_____

_____

_____

_____

_____

_____

_____

Virginia DeBolt: *Write! Social Studies*
Kagan Publishing • 1 (800) 933-2667

67

Comical History

Comic strips are usually composed of several cells, each illustrating a step in a sequence of events. In this activity, students work in teams to create a comic strip illustrating the sequence of a historical event.

at-a-glance

Cooperative Structures

• Team Project
• Blind Sequencing

Level of Thinking

• Application
• Synthesis

Multiple Intelligences

• Verbal/Linguistic
• Logical/Mathematical
• Visual/Spatial
• Interpersonal

Ideas for my class . . .	More ideas for my class . . .
• Use this activity with any historical event with a clear sequence.	• • • • • • • • • •

IDEA BANK

Team Project

Assign each team a different historical event, or assign the class the same event. For example, one event may be, "The Alamo." Tell students that they must illustrate the event in an eight cell cartoon strip, each students illustrating and writing two cells. It may be a good idea to share with the class some samples out of the newspaper. Teammates work together to plan how to summarize the event in their cartoon strip and how to divide the labor. Make two copies of the blackline for each team. Each student illustrates his or her two cells on the reproducible. When completed, teammates read the cartoon and check for accuracy and continuity.

Blind Sequencing

When teams are done with their cartoon strips, they shuffle the cells and exchange them with another team, face down. Each student gets two cells and writes his or her initials small on the back of the cells to identify the cells as his or hers. The team's goal is to sequence the cartoon cells. The challenge is students can not see or touch each other's

Virginia DeBolt: *Write! Social Studies*
Kagan Publishing • 1 (800) 933-2667

cells. Student One describe his cell and then places it face down in the middle of the team's desks or table. Student Two describes the next cell and places it before or after the first cell. This RoundRobin continues until the team has laid out their cartoon.

When all teammates agree they are properly sequenced, they flip over the cartoon and check if they are correct. They read the historical cartoon through once more. If they have a question about the sequence, they can consult with the team who created the cartoon.

Virginia DeBolt: *Write! Social Studies*
Kagan Publishing • 1 (800) 933-2667

69

Comical History

Directions: Work with your teammates to plan your historical comic strip. Cut out the cells below and give two to each teammate. Illustrate your two cells of the comic strip and write any text on the lines. When done, share your cells with your teammates.

Name _____

Name _____

Name _____

Name _____

Virginia DeBolt: *Write! Social Studies*
Kagan Publishing • 1 (800) 933-2667

Journal Topics

- What is the most important information about current history?

- What historical event would make a good movie? Why?

- Why is the town you live in a good location for a town?

- Given a time machine, where would you go and what would you do?

Virginia DeBolt: *Write! Social Studies*
Kagan Publishing • 1 (800) 933-2667

71

Political Cartoons

Political cartoonist have an uncanny ability to convey a tremendous amount of meaning with an illustration and just a few words. Sometimes the cartoon is biting, sometimes it's hilarious, often its both. In this activity, students plan their political cartoon with a partner, create it and share it with teammates.

ACTIVITY 19

at-a-glance

Materials Needed

• Markers or crayons

Cooperative Structures

• Pair Discussion
• RoundRobin

Level of Thinking

• Knowledge
• Comprehension
• Application
• Synthesis

Multiple Intelligences

• Verbal/Linguistic
• Visual/Spatial
• Interpersonal

Ideas for my class . . .	More ideas for my class . . .
Create a political cartoon about: • Current events • Events under current study • Historical events • Current political figures • Historical figures	• • • • • • • • • •

IDEA BANK

Pair Discussion

Share with the class some sample political cartoons. Most political periodicals (Time, Newsweek) and newspapers will havethem. Give students the task of creating their own political cartoon on any topic. The topic can be a current event described in the newspaper, or a past event you are learning about. Students pair up to discuss ideas for their cartoons.

Independent Write

On the reproducible, students create their political cartoon, and describe it in writing.

RoundRobin

Students take turns sharing their political cartoon with teammates.

Virginia DeBolt: *Write! Social Studies*
Kagan Publishing • 1 (800) 933-2667

Political Cartoons

Name _____ **Period** _____ **Date** _____

Directions: Fill in the topic of your political cartoon in the box below. Illustrate your political cartoon and describe it in writing.

My political cartoon on _____ .
topic

Cartoon

Describe your cartoon. _____

_____

_____

_____

_____

_____

_____

_____

_____

_____

Virginia DeBolt: *Write! Social Studies*
Kagan Publishing • 1 (800) 933-2667

73

Time Lines

When was World War I? How about World War II? Truly understanding historical events involves not only learning the details of the event, but understanding its relationship in time to other events. In this activity, develop students logical/mathematical intelligence as students work in teams to sequence events on a time line.

at-a-glance

Materials Needed

• Poster board

Cooperative Structures

• Team Project
• Teams Present

Level of Thinking

• Knowledge
• Comprehension
• Analysis
• Synthesis

Multiple Intelligences

• Verbal/Linguistic
• Logical/Mathematical
• Visual/Spatial
• Interpersonal

Ideas for my class . . .	More ideas for my class . . .
Make a time line of:	•
• Major world events	•
• Events in a century	•
• Events of an era	•
• Events in a generation	•
• Sequence of events of a war	•
• Events of a topic of study	•
• Events of a year	•
	•
	•

I D E A   B A N K

Team Project

Give the class a list of historical events. The events can be world events that occurred over the course of centuries, or can be specific events that happened over the course of a few years. Each team's job is to sequence the events and create a team time line. To do this, the team evenly divides the events. Each student is responsible for looking up the date of the event and writing a brief synopsis of the event. Students can use the reproducible to write their synopses. Students draw a large time line on foam board or butcher paper. They sequence their events and paste them on the poster. Teammates can work to illustrate their time lines.

Teams Present

When each team has completed their time line, have two teams pair up and share their time lines. Teams share the events in the sequence they occured. Each student shares the events he or she researched and summarize. Teams can post their time lines in the class to share with classmates.

Virginia DeBolt: *Write! Social Studies*
Kagan Publishing • 1 (800) 933-2667

Time Lines

Name _____ **Date** _____

Directions: Divide the events of your time line evenly among teammates. For each event, write a synopsis using the cards below. Sequence the events on your team time line.

Date _____ *Event* _____

Synopsis _____

_____

_____

_____

_____

_____

Date _____ *Event* _____

Synopsis _____

_____

_____

_____

_____

_____

Virginia DeBolt: *Write! Social Studies*
Kagan Publishing • 1 (800) 933-2667

75

News Report on History

The standard format of newspaper articles is to lead with basic information on who, what, when, where, why, and how. In addition to the five w's, the writer attempts to make the lead (the first paragraph) interesting or creative enough to entice the readers to continue reading. Information is reported in descending order of importance. If space requirements demand, the article can be cut, at the end, where the least important information is written. In this activity, students write a newspaper article on any social studies topic.

at-a-glance

Materials Needed

• computers with newsletter publishing software, if possible

Cooperative Structures

• RoundTable
• RoundRobin

Level of Thinking

• Synthesis
• Evaluation

Multiple Intelligences

• Verbal/Linguistic
• Visual/Spatial
• Interpersonal

IDEA BANK

Ideas for my class...	More ideas for my class...
Write an article on: • Civil War • Battle of the Alamo • First moon landing • Crusades • Black Plague • Opening of Sistine Chapel • Louisiana Purchase • Discovery of gold • First Olympic games	• • • • • • • • •

RoundTable

Assign the class a newspaper topic relating to your topic of study. For example, students may write an article on the Louisiana Purchase. Have each team take out a sheet of paper, write the topic at the top and write the five W's evenly spaced down the side. See graphics below.

Louisiana Purchase
Who
What
When
Where
Why

Students pass around the paper, each in turn adding important information. For example, under the "Who" column, Student One may add, "Thomas Jefferson is President. Student Two may add, "Napoleon is France's ruler."

Independent Write

When students have the five W's filled in about the event, they write their articles on the reproducible using the information they generated.

RoundRobin

Students share their newspaper articles with teammates.

Virginia DeBolt: *Write! Social Studies*
Kagan Publishing • 1 (800) 933-2667

News Report on History

Name _____ **Date** _____

Directions: Write a newspaper story about a social studies topic. Give your newspaper a name. Include a headline and an illustration.

_____
Newspaper Name

_____
Headline

Picture

Virginia DeBolt: *Write! Social Studies*
Kagan Publishing • 1 (800) 933-2667

77

Battles Over the Bill of Rights

The battle lines over the Bill of Rights are drawn and redrawn again and again. The news is filled with articles about banning pornography from the internet, computer chips that allow parents to keep selected television programs from appearing on their home TV, the right of citizens to carry weapons, and prayer in public schools. In this activity, students take a stand on issues dealing with the Bill of Rights.

ACTIVITY 22

at-a-glance

Cooperative Structures

• Agreement Circles
• RoundRobin

Level of Thinking

• Evaluation

Multiple Intelligences

• Verbal/Linguistic
• Bodily/Kinesthetic
• Interpersonal

Ideas for my class . . .	More ideas for my class . . .
Sample value statements:	•
• The police should use computers to learn everything about a person.	•
	•
	•
	•
• Songwriters should say whatever they want in a song.	•
	•
	•
• Accused criminals don't deserve lawyers appointed at government expense.	•
	•

IDEA BANK

Agreement Circles

Have the class form one large circle. Stand in the middle and pose a value statement relating to the Bill of Rights. For example, "Citizens have the right to carry guns." Or, "The school principal should lead the school in a prayer every morning." Students who strongly disagree with your statement don't move. Students who strongly agree, step into the center of the circle, near you. Students who agree or disagree somewhat, step in to the center of the circle in proportion to their agreement. Have students pair up with students who share the same opinion and a different opinion to discuss the issue and how it relates to the Bill of Rights.

Independent Write

Students write a paper on the reproducible stating their belief on the issue and their interpretation of the Bill of Rights.

RoundRobin

Students share their writing with teammates.

Virginia DeBolt: *Write! Social Studies*
Kagan Publishing • 1 (800) 933-2667

Battles Over the Bill of Rights

Bill of Rights
1.
2.
3.
4.
5.
6.
7.
8.
9.
10.

Name _____ **Date** _____

Directions: Fill in the issue in the box below. Describe your stand on the issue.
Use evidence from a specific amendment to support your view.

How I feel about _____ .
                                            topic

Describe your viewpoint _____

_____

_____

_____

_____

_____

_____

_____

_____

_____

_____

_____

_____

_____

_____

_____

_____

_____

_____

_____

_____

_____

_____

Virginia DeBolt: *Write! Social Studies*
Kagan Publishing • 1 (800) 933-2667

79

A Critical Look at History

Take a critical look at history by exploring an event from all angles—or at least six different angles. In this activity, students are led through six questions about the event, then write a coherent essay about the event.

Cooperative Structures

• Think-Write-Pair
• RoundRobin

Level of Thinking

• Knowledge
• Comprehension
• Application
• Analysis
• Synthesis
• Evaluation

Multiple Intelligences

• Verbal/Linguistic
• Logical/Mathematical
• Interpersonal

Ideas for my class . . .	More ideas for my class . . .
Take a critical look at: • Current events • Events in the chapter under study • Election year events • Supreme Court decisions	• • • • • • • • • •

I D E A B A N K

Think-Write-Pair

Give the class an historical event relating to the topic of study. For example, the Great Depression. Give the class the first task on the reproducible. "Describe the Great Depression as well as you can." Have students think about the topic for 15-30 seconds, then start writing on the reproducible. After ample writing time, have students pair up and share what they wrote. Give students a little time to jot down any additional ideas from their partner. Then, give the class the second task on the reproducible and have them think, write and share their ideas again. Continue this process until you have explored the event from all six angles.

Independent Write

Have students write about the event, exploring it from all angles.

RoundRobin

Students take turns sharing their writing with teammates.

Virginia DeBolt: *Write! Social Studies*
Kagan Publishing • 1 (800) 933-2667

A Critical Look at History

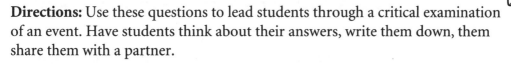

Directions: Use these questions to lead students through a critical examination of an event. Have students think about their answers, write them down, them share them with a partner.

1. Describe the Event.

What happened? Who was involved? When did it happen? Where did it happen?

2. Compare the Event.

What other event does this remind you of?

3. Associate the Event.

How is this event related to your own life?

4. Apply the Event.

What can we learn from this event? How can you apply it to the present?

5. Analyze the Event.

What is unique about the event? What relationships can you uncover?

6. Argue the Event.

Should it have happened? Why or why not? Could it have been avoided? How?

Virginia DeBolt: *Write! Social Studies*
Kagan Publishing • 1 (800) 933-2667

81

Re-inventing the Government

In order to vote, we must register well in advance, take time out of our schedule to go to an authorized location, stand in line, provide proper identification, wait for our name to be located, and then we can actually vote. Why can't we just... In this activity, students re-invent the government, or at least a part of the government.

ACTIVITY

24

at-a-glance

Cooperative Structures

• Team Discussion
• Simultaneous Chalkboard Share
• RoundRobin

Level of Thinking

• Application
• Synthesis
• Evaluation

Multiple Intelligences

• Verbal/Linguistic
• Logical/Mathematical
• Interpersonal
• Intrapersonal

Ideas for my class . . .	More ideas for my class . . .
Re-invent:	•
• The voting process	•
• Tax laws	•
• The prison system	•
• Public education	•
• Passing a law	•
• Speed limit	•
• Military regulations	•
	•
	•

I D E A   B A N K

Team Discussion

Announce the part of the government that needs to be "re-invented." For example, "How do we re-invent the voting process?" Have students work in teams to discuss alternatives. Have one student on the team record the team's best ideas.

Simultaneous Chalkboard Share

Send one representative from each team to an assigned part of the chalkboard to write the team's best idea(s). Have each team share their ideas with the class.

Independent Write

Using ideas that teammates or classmates shared, students write their plan to re-invent the part of government.

RoundRobin

Students take turns sharing their plans to re-invent the government with teammates.

82

Virginia DeBolt: *Write! Social Studies*
Kagan Publishing • 1 (800) 933-2667

Re-inventing the Government

Name _____ **Date** _____

Directions: Fill in the part of government that you will re-invent in the blank below. Write a plan to re-invent that part of the government. Be prepared to share your plan with teammates.

My plan to re-invent _____ .
topic

Describe your plan to re-invent the government. _____

_____

_____

_____

_____

_____

_____

_____

_____

_____

_____

_____

_____

_____

_____

_____

_____

_____

_____

_____

Virginia DeBolt: *Write! Social Studies*
Kagan Publishing • 1 (800) 933-2667

83

Visualize History

When you hear the word Hiroshima, what do you visualize? Can you illustrate what you imagine? In this activity, develop students' visual/spatial intelligence and make history become vivid by having students draw and describe images that come to mind from historical events.

ACTIVITY 25

at-a-glance

Cooperative Structures

• Think-Pair-Share
• RoundRobin

Level of Thinking

• Application
• Synthesis

Multiple Intelligences

• Verbal/Linguistic
• Visual/Spatial
• Interpersonal

Ideas for my class . . .	More ideas for my class . . .
What image comes to mind when you hear the word(s): • Historical events: Gettysburg Address, 21st Amendment, New Deal • Social Studies concepts: Inalienable rights, campaign, patronage, embargo, emancipation	• • • • • • • • •

IDEA BANK

Think-Pair-Share

After learning about a historical event, have students close their eyes and visualize the event. Take the Boston Tea Party as an example: "Close your eyes. It's the evening of December 16, 1773. You are in the Boston Harbor. What do you see?" Give students plenty of time to visualize what they see. Have students pair up and discuss their visual images. Select several students to share their visualization with the class.

Independent Write

Have students draw a representation of what they saw on the reproducible and describe the scene as vividly as they can.

RoundRobin

In teams, students take turns sharing their illustrations and reading their descriptions.

Virginia DeBolt: *Write! Social Studies*
Kagan Publishing • 1 (800) 933-2667

Visualizing History

Name _____ **Date** _____

Directions: Fill in the historical event in the box below. Describe your visual image of the event. Be prepared to share your illustration and writing with teammates.

My visual image of ————————————————————— .
topic

Illustration

Describe your image. ————————————————————

_____

_____

_____

_____

_____

_____

_____

_____

_____

Virginia DeBolt: *Write! Social Studies*
Kagan Publishing • 1 (800) 933-2667

85

Résumé Writer

Do students know that Harry S. Truman was a haberdasher? That Jimmy Carter was a peanut farmer? How do a person's experiences prepare him or her to become a significant figure in history? Rachel Carson changed the world–what was on her résumé? In this activity, students research a historical character in pairs and write a résumé for that character.

at-a-glance

Cooperative Structures

• Pair Project
• Pairs Present

Level of Thinking

• Application
• Analysis
• Synthesis

Multiple Intelligences

• Verbal/Linguistic
• Logical/Mathematical
• Interpersonal

Ideas for my class . . .	More ideas for my class . . .
Write a résumé for:	•
• Presidents of the U.S.	•
• World leaders	•
• Famous women	•
• Civil rights leaders	•
• Political figures	•
• Famous African	•
Americans	•
• Famous Hispanics	•
• Famous Asians	•

IDEA BANK

Pair Project

Assign each pair a significant historical figure about whom there will be sufficient information available in the text or library to write a résumé. If possible, use figures relating to the topic of study. The entire class can also be assigned the same figure to research. Using the reproducible, pairs work together to create a résumé for the historical figure.

Pairs Present

If pairs research a different historical figure, have them pair up with another pair to share their person's résumé. Pairs can do several rounds of sharing each time with a different pair audience. This way, pairs practice sharing their character various times and learn about different historical characters. If the entire class is researching the same character, the pair can share with the other pair on their team.

86

Virginia DeBolt: *Write! Social Studies*
Kagan Publishing • 1 (800) 933-2667

Résumé Writer

Names _____ Date _____

_____

Directions: Write the résumé of an historical character.

Résumé

Name _____

Address _____

Occupational Objectives _____

_____

_____

Skills _____

_____

_____

Experience
Date   *Experience*

_____

_____

_____

_____

_____

_____

_____

Education
Date   *Education*

_____

_____

_____

Court Case Simulation

ACTIVITY

27

at-a-glance

The decisions of some landmark court cases have altered the history of the United States. In this activity, students work in teams to research a landmark court cases write a script for the case, rehearse it as a team and perform it for the class. By simulating a court case, students become actively engaged in the learning process, and get an insight to the nation's judicial system.

Cooperative Structures

- Team Project
- Teams Present
- RoundRobin

Level of Thinking

- Knowledge
- Comprehension
- Application
- Analysis
- Synthesis
- Evaluation

Multiple Intelligences

- Verbal/Linguistic
- Logical/Mathematical
- Visual/Spatial
- Bodily/Kinesthetic
- Interpersonal
- Intrapersonal

Ideas for my class . . .	More ideas for my class . . .
Court cases:	•
• Brown vs. Board of Education	•
• Roe vs. Wade	•
• Lindbergh trial	•
• Rosenbergs' case	•
• Scopes trial	•
• Miranda case	•
	•
	•

I D E A

B A N K

Team Project

Select a court case that is relevant to the time period or theme being studied. Decide how many students would be necessary to simulate the case. For example, you may need a judge, a defendant, defense attorneys, a prosecutor, a witness and so on. Each case will vary. Write the names of the participants on the board. Announce the topic to the class and have students form groups corresponding to the number of participants needed. Groups of 6-8 work well.

Tell students they must recreate the court case and give them a time limit. Each student is given one of the roles on the chalkboard and all students must be involved in the simulation. Teammates work together to research the court case and decide how they will simulate it. The more trial records and resources available to students, the more accurate it will be. Teams write a script for their simulation and rehearse it. This project may be on-going for several days.

88

Virginia DeBolt: *Write! Social Studies*
Kagan Publishing • 1 (800) 933-2667

Teams Present

When students are prepared or the due date has arrived, teams put on their court case simulation for the class.

Independent Write

After students have seen the court cases on the topic, students write their reflections on the case and its significance on the reproducible.

RoundRobin

In teams, students take turns reading their court cases reflections.

Virginia DeBolt: *Write! Social Studies*
Kagan Publishing • 1 (800) 933-2667

89

Court Case Simulation

Name _____ **Date** _____

Directions: Fill in the title of your court case in the box below. Write a summary of the case, the significance of the case and how you feel about it.

My synthesis of _____ .

court case

Summary of case _____

_____

_____

_____

_____

_____

_____

_____

Significance of case _____

_____

_____

_____

_____

_____

_____

_____

How I feel _____

_____

_____

_____

Virginia DeBolt: *Write! Social Studies*
Kagan Publishing • 1 (800) 933-2667

Journal Topics

- Write five Trivial Pursuit questions based on today's chapter.

- Take an event from today's chapter and write a brief fictional account about it.

- Pick a theme song for a character from today's chapter. Explain why it fits.

- Suppose you were present at a historical event from today's chapter. How would you feel?

Virginia DeBolt: *Write! Social Studies*
Kagan Publishing • 1 (800) 933-2667

91

State Your Opinion

In this activity, students explore their opinions on a controversial topic related to the social studies theme. Students write an opinion paper and share it with teammates.

at-a-glance

Cooperative Structures

• Value Line
• RoundRobin

Level of Thinking

• Application
• Evaluation

Multiple Intelligences

• Verbal/Linguistic
• Bodily/Kinesthetic
• Interpersonal
• Intrapersonal

Ideas for my class...	More ideas for my class...
What's your opinion on: • Driving age • Movie ratings • Academic testing • Gang graffiti • Dress codes • Music • School food	• • • • • • • • •

IDEA BANK

Value Line

Make a controversial value statement related to your social studies theme that will spark students' interest. For example, when examining the theme *individuals, groups and institutions,* a relevant statement might be: "Students should wear uniforms to school." Or when examining the theme *science, technology and society,* a controversial statement might be: "A rating system should be set up on the internet and children should not be allowed to enter 'R' or 'X' rated web sites." Students take a stand on an imaginary line in the classroom that has "strongly disagree" on one end and "strongly agree" on the other end.

Have students turn to a partner in line and discuss their opinion on the issue. Then, fold the line in half so students who strongly agree are facing students who strongly disagree. Have students pair up and discuss their opposing opinions.

Independent Write

Once students have discussed their opinion on the issue and have heard the counter argument, they are ready to write a paper in defense of their position.

RoundRobin

Students take turns reading their paper to teammates.

Virginia DeBolt: *Write! Social Studies*
Kagan Publishing • 1 (800) 933-2667

State Your Opinion

Name _____ **Date** _____

Directions: Fill in the issue you are exploring in the box below. Describe your opinion on the issue and three reasons why you feel the way you do.

My opinion on _____ .
                                    value issue

My opinion _____

_____

_____

_____

_____

_____

_____

_____

_____

_____

_____

_____

_____

_____

_____

_____

_____

_____

_____

_____

Virginia DeBolt: *Write! Social Studies*
Kagan Publishing • 1 (800) 933-2667

93

Everything Has a History

Did you know that Thomas Edison was not the inventor of electric light? Joseph Wilson Swan from Britain invented a filament lamp in 1878, nearly a year before Edison. In this activity, students research the unique history of a topic, write a summary and share it with teammates.

ACTIVITY 29

at-a-glance

Cooperative Structures

• Pair Project
• RoundRobin

Level of Thinking

• Comprehension
• Application
• Synthesis

Multiple Intelligences

• Verbal/Linguistic

Ideas for my class . . .	More ideas for my class . . .
What is the history of:	•
• Light bulb	•
• Milking machine	•
• Refrigerator	•
• Democracy	•
• Prejudice	•
• Golf	•
• Basketball	•
• Two party system	•
• Welfare	•

IDEA BANK

Pair Project

Announce the research topic to the class. For example, "What is the history of the television?" Or, "What is the history of the presidency?" Students work in pairs to research the history of the assigned topic. Each pair can also be assigned a different topic to research.

Independent Write

After pairs have ample information on the topic, they split up and each individual writes his or her own history summary on the reproducible.

RoundRobin

Students take turns reading their summaries to teammates. If you have pairs research different topics, have students switch teams to share so students learn about the history of various topics. Students can switch teams several times to do several rounds of sharing. Consider allowing students to revise after sharing the first time.

Virginia DeBolt: *Write! Social Studies*
Kagan Publishing • 1 (800) 933-2667

Everything Has a History

Name _____ **Date** _____

Directions: Fill in the topic in the box below. Write a brief history of the object. Be prepared to share it with teammates.

> *The History of* _____ .
> topic

_____

_____

_____

_____

_____

_____

_____

_____

_____

_____

_____

_____

_____

_____

_____

_____

_____

_____

_____

_____

_____

_____

_____

_____

Virginia DeBolt: *Write! Social Studies*
Kagan Publishing • 1 (800) 933-2667

95

Ecosystem Journey

Developing an awareness of other geographic areas and ecosystems is an important social studies goal. In this activity, take students through an imaginary journey through an ecosystem, and write about the ecosystem.

ACTIVITY 30

at-a-glance

Cooperative Structures

- Think-Pair-Write
- RoundRobin

Level of Thinking

- Synthesis

Multiple Intelligences

- Verbal/Linguistic
- Logical/Mathematical
- Visual/Spatial
- Interpersonal
- Intrapersonal
- Naturalist

Ideas for my class . . .	More ideas for my class . . .
Explore the ecosystem:	•
• Desert	•
• Steppe	•
• Wetland	•
• Rain forest	•
• Marsh	•
• Arctic	•
• Prairie	•
• Wooded mountain lake	•
• Island	•

IDEA BANK

Think-Pair-Write

If you are learning about the rainforest, take students through an imaginary journey through the sights, sounds, smells of the rainforest. Have students close their eyes and start describing the rainforest. With their eyes still closed, ask students what animals they see. Give them 10-15 seconds of think time, then have them pair with a partner to discuss what animals they saw and what they looked like. On a separate sheet of paper, let students write for a couple minutes about the animals in the ecosystem. Continue this process with the birds, water, weather conditions and so on until students have shared and written about the various aspects of the ecosystem.

Independent Write

On the reproducible, students write about their imaginary journey through the ecosystem.

RoundRobin

In turn, students share their writing with teammates.

Virginia DeBolt: *Write! Social Studies*
Kagan Publishing • 1 (800) 933-2667

Ecosystem Journey

Directions: Fill in the ecosystem in the box below. Describe your imaginary journey through the ecosystem. Include accurate details about the things you would see, hear, feel, smell and taste. Complete the journey with a conclusion about the suitability of the area as a place where you might like to live.

My journey in _____ .

ecosystem

_____

_____

_____

_____

_____

_____

_____

_____

_____

_____

_____

_____

_____

_____

_____

_____

_____

_____

_____

_____

_____

Virginia DeBolt: *Write! Social Studies*
Kagan Publishing • 1 (800) 933-2667

97

Sports Broadcast

People are fascinated by sports. Students are no exception. Fans go crazy watching sports in person, on television, and even learning about the sport on the radio. In this activity, students become sports writers and write a rousing description of a sport or event of the past or that of another culture.

ACTIVITY

31

at-a-glance

Cooperative Structure

• RoundRobin

Level of Thinking

• Application

Multiple Intelligences

• Verbal/Linguistic
• Visual/Spatial
• Bodily/Kinesthetic
• Interpersonal

IDEA BANK

Ideas for my class...	More ideas for my class...
Write a broadcast for: • Medieval jousting tournament • Olympic games in Ancient Greece • First American football game • Native American game with netted sticks (lacrosse)	• • • • • • • • •

Independent Write

After learning about a sport of the past or of another culture, students work independently to write the script of a radio or television broadcast.

RoundRobin

Each student in turn reads his or her script to teammates. After each reader is finished, teammates offer appreciation, then suggestions on volume, clarity and content.

Independent Write

Students can revise their broadcast based on teammates' feedback.

RoundRobin

Have students switch teams and share their sports broadcast with new teammates.

98

Virginia DeBolt: *Write! Social Studies*
Kagan Publishing • 1 (800) 933-2667

Sports Broadcast

Name _____ **Date** _____

Directions: Fill in the sport of another time or culture in the box below. Write a radio or television broadcast about the sporting event. Be prepared to share your broadcast with teammates.

My broadcast on _____ .
                                              sport

_____

_____

_____

_____

_____

_____

_____

_____

_____

_____

_____

_____

_____

_____

_____

_____

_____

_____

_____

_____

_____

_____

_____

Virginia DeBolt: *Write! Social Studies*
Kagan Publishing • 1 (800) 933-2667

99

Viewpoints

What are Thomas Jefferson's views on voting rights? What evidence do you have to support your claim? In this activity, students write a thesis sentence about a historical figure's view on an issue and support their claim with specific evidence.

at-a-glance

Cooperative Structure

• Pair Project

Level of Thinking

• Comprehension
• Application
• Evaluation
• Synthesis

Multiple Intelligences

• Verbal/Linguistic
• Interpersonal

Ideas for my class . . .	More ideas for my class . . .
Write about: • Adolph Hitler's views on individual rights • Lech Walesa's views on representative democracy • Golda Meir's views on Palestinian homeland • Susan B. Anthony's views on women's rights	• • • • • • • • •

I D E A B A N K

Pair Project

Assign the class a historical character and ask them what the person's view is on a related issue. For example, "What's Frederick Douglass' view of slavery?" Pairs work to write a thesis sentence on the reproducible. A good thesis statement takes a stand on the issue and alludes to the supporting evidence that follows. For example, after reviewing Douglass' history students may write, "Frederick Douglass was adamantly opposed to slavery as seen by his escapes to freedom, his public speeches against slavery, and his abolition publications." Partners fill in the details of the thesis supporting evidence in the reproducible. For example, in Evidence 1, students take notes detailing Douglass' two escape attempts; Evidence 2, students take notes about Douglass' anti-slavery speeches; Evidence 3, students take notes about Douglass' narrative and his own newspaper.

Independent Write

Students use their notes to write an essay on the person's viewpoint. The essay can be shared with teammates or turned in for feedback.

100

Virginia DeBolt: *Write! Social Studies*
Kagan Publishing • 1 (800) 933-2667

Viewpoints

Names _____ **Date** _____

_____

Directions: Fill in the person's view on the issue in the box below. With your partner, write a thesis on the topic and take notes on the evidence to support your claim. Use these notes to write an essay on the topic.

_____ *view on* _____ .
    person   *issue*

THESIS

_____
_____
_____
_____
_____

EVIDENCE 1   *EVIDENCE 2*   *EVIDENCE 3*

Virginia DeBolt: *Write! Social Studies*
Kagan Publishing • 1 (800) 933-2667

101

Advantages and Disadvantages

ACTIVITY

33

at-a-glance

There are many expressions labeling the dilemma of dealing with the dual nature of decision making. We say, "You have to take the good with the bad." Or "There are two sides to every coin." Or, "The ends justify the means." Or, "This is a gray area." In this activity, students list the advantages and disadvantages on the issue, then write a paper taking a stand.

Cooperative Structures

• Pairs Compare
• RoundRobin

Level of Thinking

• Analysis
• Synthesis
• Evaluation

Multiple Intelligences

• Verbal/Linguistic
• Logical/Mathematical
• Visual/Spatial
• Interpersonal

Ideas for my class . . .	*More ideas for my class . . .*
What are the advantages and disadvantages of:	•
• Affirmative action	•
• Legalization of concealed weapons	•
• State lotteries	•
• Death penalty	•
• Trial by jury	•

I D E A   B A N K

Pairs Compare

Announce a topic related to the topic of study that has advantages and disadvantages. For example, "Should we have the death penalty?" Students work in pairs to list the advantages and disadvantages on the reproducible. After a predetermined amount of time or when students can think of no more ideas, they unite with the other pair on their team and compare advantages and disadvantages. Pairs record any additional ideas from the other pair. As a team, students see if they can think of any more advantages or disadvantages.

Independent Write

Using the advantages and disadvantages gleaned from the previous activity, students work independently to write an essay. Tell them to use only the three most important advantages/disadvantages in their paper.

RoundRobin

In teams, students share their essays.

102

Virginia DeBolt: *Write! Social Studies*
Kagan Publishing • 1 (800) 933-2667

Advantages and Disadvantages

Name _____ **Date** _____

Directions: Fill in the topic in the blank below. With a partner write down as many advantages and disadvantages as you can think of. Then work with another pair to compare your ideas.

On a separate sheet write an essay taking a stand on the issue. Your writing should include: 1) introduction and the main idea, 2) the disadvantages, 3) the advantages, and 4) a recommendation or opinion on the main idea.

> *The advantages and disadvantages of* _____.
> *issue*

Advantages	Disadvantages

Virginia DeBolt: *Write! Social Studies*
Kagan Publishing • 1 (800) 933-2667

103

Believe It or Not!

Did you know President Bush had some wooden teeth? Actually, he didn't, but George Washington really did. In this activity, students work in teams to write some unbelievable truths and some believable fibs to see if they can fool their classmates with interesting history trivia.

Cooperative Structures

- Find-the-Fiction
- Team Project

Level of Thinking

- Comprehension
- Application
- Synthesis

Multiple Intelligences

- Verbal/Linguistic
- Interpersonal

Ideas for my class . . .	More ideas for my class . . .
Write about true but unbelievable:	•
• Laws	•
• Cultural practices	•
• Facts about a particular time period	•
• Inventions	•
• Court cases	•
• Historical events	•
• Famous figures	•

I D E A

B A N K

Find-the-Fiction

Have each student write three statements relating to the topic, two unbelievable truths and one believable fib. Students also write the "Why" behind the unbelievable truths. For example, if studying China, a student might write: "Chinese women once bound their feet to keep them from growing. This forced women to hobble about for a lifetime on deformed feet. Under "Why" the student might write: "Small feet were considered beautiful for women." Students read their three statements to teammates and teammates try to find the fib.

Students then read the "Why" behind the unbelievable truths.

Team Project

After teammates have each shared their statements, teams pick out their favorite two truths and their favorite believable fib.

Find-the-Fiction

Each team presents their three statements to the class. Students on the other teams put their heads together to try to find the fib and can vote by holding up a number card or fingers corresponding to the statement that is a fib.

Virginia DeBolt: *Write! Social Studies*
Kagan Publishing • 1 (800) 933-2667

Believe It or Not!

Name _____ **Date** _____

Directions: Write three statements about the assigned topic, two unbelievable truths and one believable fib. For the two unbelievable truths, describe why they are true. In random order, read your statements to your teammates. See if they can find the fib.

Unbelievable truth _____
_____
_____

Why it's true _____
_____
_____

Unbelievable truth _____
_____
_____

Why it's true _____
_____
_____

Believable fib _____
_____
_____
_____
_____

Virginia DeBolt: *Write! Social Studies*
Kagan Publishing • 1 (800) 933-2667

105

Collect Artifacts

People have all sorts of cultural and historical artifacts at home: antique tools, foreign currency, carved ivory, flint arrow points, World War II mortar shells. In this activity, students write about their artifact and bring it in to share with the class.

ACTIVITY

35

at-a-glance

Cooperative Structure

• RoundRobin

Level of Thinking

• Application
• Synthesis

Multiple Intelligences

• Verbal/Linguistic
• Logical/Mathematical
• Spatial/Visual
• Bodily/Kinesthetic
• Musical/Rhythmic
• Interpersonal

Ideas for my class . . .	More ideas for my class . . .
Share artifacts from: • Native Americans • The Old West • Early settlers in the area • Other cultures • Ancient civilizations	• • • • • • • • • •

IDEA BANK

Independent Write

Have students bring an artifact from home from another culture or time period to share with the class. Encourage students to get creative with what they bring in and describe. For example, a student may bring in Brazilian maracas to share music with the class. On the reproducible, students write a description of the artifact including its time period and uses. For example, the student describing the maracas may write how the word maraca comes from the Portuguese word maracá and how Portuguese is the language spoken in Brazil and how the original maracas were dried gourds with gourd seeds or pebbles, shaken to create rhythm. Students may have to do some research to find out more about their artifact.

RoundRobin

In teams, students take turns sharing their artifacts and reading their descriptions. An alternative is to have each student share their artifact with the class. The artifacts can be passed around or put in the class "Artifact Museum" for the week.

106

Virginia DeBolt: *Write! Social Studies*
Kagan Publishing • 1 (800) 933-2667

Collect Artifacts

Name _____ **Date** _____

Directions: Fill in the name of your artifact in the box below. Answer the questions about your artifact. Be prepared to share your artifact with classmates.

My artifact is _____ .
artifact name

What does it look and feel like? _____
_____
_____
_____

Where is it from? _____
_____
_____
_____

What is it used for? _____
_____
_____
_____

What time period is it from? _____
_____
_____
_____
_____

Virginia DeBolt: *Write! Social Studies*
Kagan Publishing • 1 (800) 933-2667

107

Current Events

Current events are an old social studies favorite to keep students informed on the goings-on in their community and in the world. The problem is, they take too long! Use this more practical, cooperative format to keep students well-informed about current events.

Ideas for my class . . .	More ideas for my class . . .
Write current events on: • Daily newspaper articles • Magazines • Periodicals • Past events	• • • • • • • • • • •

IDEA BANK

Cooperative Structure

• RoundRobin

Level of Thinking

• Analysis
• Evaluation

Multiple Intelligences

• Verbal/Linguistic
• Interpersonal
• Intrapersonal

Independent Write

Have students pick a newspaper or periodical article of interest for their current event. Students read their articles and write a summary on the reproducible.

RoundRobin

To share current events, students normally read their summaries to the class. If each student takes only two minutes to share their current event with the class, in a class of 30, it would take over an hour to share current events. Instead, have students take turns reading their current events in small teams. In a team of four, students can share their current event and hear three other current events in just eight minutes. Students are more active listeners as the setting is more intimate. With this format, you can make current events a regular part of social studies.

108

Virginia DeBolt: *Write! Social Studies*
Kagan Publishing • 1 (800) 933-2667

Current Events

Name _____ **Date** _____

Directions: Pick out a recent article in a newspaper or magazine. Read the article, and write a summary and your feelings below. Staple the article to this paper. Be prepared to share your current event with classmates.

Article title _____

_____ Date _____

Newspaper or magazine _____

Section _____

Summary of article _____

_____

_____

_____

_____

_____

_____

_____

_____

_____

_____

_____

_____

_____

_____

_____

How I feel about the issue _____

_____

_____

_____

_____

Virginia DeBolt: *Write! Social Studies*
Kagan Publishing • 1 (800) 933-2667

109

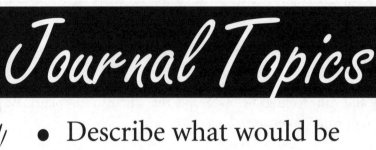

Journal Topics

- Describe what would be different if the event never happened or the figure never lived.

- Explain the importance of an explorer or discoverer.

- Describe buildings or artifacts of the culture discussed in this chapter.

- Compare two cultures, governments, historical figures or historical events.

- Tell how understanding the importance of a resource effects the use of it.

110

Virginia DeBolt: *Write! Social Studies*
Kagan Publishing • 1 (800) 933-2667

Cooperative Learning Structures

The directions regarding the structures used in the writing activities were specific for that activity. In this section of the book, you will find a more general description of the structures, one which may help you see how you can apply it in other ways in your classroom.

Dr. Spencer Kagan's book *Kagan Cooperative Learning* is the definitive resource and guide to cooperative learning structures. He has designed and refined over one hundred cooperative learning strategies, each one carefully planned to include the principles of cooperative learning. Those principles are:

- **Positive Interdependence**
- **Individual Accountability**
- **Equal Participation**
- **Simultaneous Interaction**

Using cooperative learning structures helps you achieve success with cooperative learning because the basic principles to successful cooperative learning are "built in." The marvelous thing about the structures is that they are content free. If you use an activity from this book involving Think-Pair-Share or RoundRobin with writing content, you can use these cooperative structures equally well with any content. From kindergarten to graduate school, from astrophysics to plumbing repair, cooperative learning structures are helpful tools to build effective learning experiences.

Virginia DeBolt: *Write! Social Studies*
Kagan Publishing • 1 (800) 933-2667

111

Agreement Circles

Students demonstrate their agreement or disagreement with an issue by physically locating themselves in the Agreement Circle. Agreement Circles is a great way to have students explore their own values as well as those of classmates.

Tell students to form a large circle in open space in the classroom. Stand in the middle of the circle and make a value statement. The statement must be worded so that students can respond with a measure of agreement or disagreement. Sample statements: "The needs of a tiny, obscure species should not be placed ahead of the needs of thousands of people." Or, "It makes good sense to transplant baboon hearts into humans with bad hearts." After hearing the statement, students decide whether or not they agree with the statement. Students who strongly disagree with your statement do not move from the perimeter of the circle. Students who strongly agree with your statement move to the center of the circle, near you. Students who disagree somewhat or see both sides of the issue, step into the center of the circle in proportion to their agreement.

After students have taken their new positions in the Agreement Circle, pair them in these ways:
- "Pair with someone near you who agrees with your position. Talk about your opinion on the statement."
- "Pair with someone away from you who disagrees with your position. Talk about your opinion on the statement."
- "Pair with someone who sees both sides of the issue. Talk about your opinion on the statement."

Students can develop their own value statements on the issue and take turns leading Agreement.

Virginia DeBolt: *Write! Social Studies*
Kagan Publishing • 1 (800) 933-2667

Blind Sequencing

Teams work to sequence cards in their proper order, but there is a catch—each student gets his or her own cards, and no one else can see what's on them. Blind Sequence creates strong interdependence among teammates and fosters sequential thinking.

The team is given a set of cards which depict some sort of sequence. Social studies examples may be cards depicting the sequence of events of a war or cards each with one amendment of the Bill of Rights. The cards are given to the team face down so students can not see what's on the cards. The cards are shuffled face down and evenly distributed among teammates. Each student writes his or her initials or some sort of unique identifying on the back of the cards. This is done to identify students' cards since only the original card holder may touch or sequence his or her cards. Students pick up their cards and study the content. Teammates take turns describing the content of their cards. The team discusses the sequence, and attempt to properly sequence the cards face down on the desks or table. Students can not lay down their cards until teammates agree on the sequence. If there is any confusion, students may peek at their own cards and describe them to teammates. When the team thinks they have the proper sequence, they turn over their cards and check the sequence.

Virginia DeBolt: *Write! Social Studies*
Kagan Publishing • 1 (800) 933-2667

113

Find-the-Fiction

Students share three statements with teammates. Their challenge is to find which of the three statements is a fib. Find-the-Fiction is a fun way to discover interesting facts about the content.

Each student on the team writes down three statements relating to the content, two unbelievable truths and one believable fib. The goal is to write a fib that teammates will believe to be true and a fact that teammates will believe to be a fib. One students reads her statements to teammates in random order. Teammates discuss the statements and decide which of the three is a fib. Some research may be involved. Teammates guess which statement is a fib. If they guess correctly, the fibber applauds teammates. If teammates guess incorrectly, they applaud the fibber. The reader can go over her unbelievable truths and state why they're true.

Find-the-Fiction can also be played as a class. One student or a team reads his or her statements to the class. Teams put their heads together to reach consensus on the fib. They vote on the fib with a show of fingers or number cards corresponding to the fib.

Virginia DeBolt: *Write! Social Studies*
Kagan Publishing • 1 (800) 933-2667

Jigsaw Problem Solving

Students are each responsible for learning part of the material, then sharing it with teammates. Jigsaw creates strong positive interdependence.

Jigsaw is a division of labor structure. A team is divided so that each teammate is responsible for one part of the material. The materials is usually divided into four parts. Students meet with others who are assigned the same material and work together to team the material and plan how to present the material to teammates. Teammates are reunited and each student teaches teammates his or her part of the learning material.

Virginia DeBolt: *Write! Social Studies*
Kagan Publishing • 1 (800) 933-2667

115

Structure 5

Pair Discussion

Students pair up to discuss any topic. Pair Discussion provides an intimate setting that promotes active discussion and listening.

Pair Discussion is simply two students pairing up for a brief time during which they discuss the matter under study. They might discuss the best way to do something, the best answer to a question, the steps in a process, or the meaning of a vocabulary word.

Structure 6

Pair Project

Students work together with a partner to complete a project. Pairs provide students the opportunity to collaborate efforts, yet are small enough to maximize participation.

In Pair Project, two students pair up to work on an assigned project. The project can involve any type of pair work: creating products, doing research, solving problems, conducting experiments, inventing new machines. It is a good idea to create a project that neither student could do alone or to structure the project so that both students must contribute. This way, students are both accountable for their contribution and no one student can do all the work.

Virginia DeBolt: *Write! Social Studies*
Kagan Publishing • 1 (800) 933-2667

Pairs Compare

Students work in pairs to generate a list of ideas, then pairs compare their ideas with another pair. Pairs compare is a great way to generate and share lots of ideas.

Students pair up to make a list of ideas related to the topic. A social studies example may be, "List all the advantages and disadvantages of capitalism." Partners take turns listing their ideas. After designated amount of time, pairs get together and compare their ideas. They go through their lists to make sure the other pair came up with the same ideas. Partners record any additional ideas the other pair came up with. The team then works together to see if they can come up with any new or better ideas.

Pairs Present

Pairs present their project with another pair, team, or the class. Pairs Present is an excellent way for students to share information with classmates and hone their presentation skills.

When two students have worked together on a project, assignment or experiment and have a product or results to share with the class, use a Pairs Present. The two should participate equally in the presentation, and in some way be held individually accountable for knowing all the information involved in the assignment.

Virginia DeBolt: *Write! Social Studies*
Kagan Publishing • 1 (800) 933-2667

117

Structure 9

RallyTable

In pairs, students take turns writing. RallyTable is a quick and easy way to generate and record ideas or write pair papers. The turn-taking ensures equal participation.

RallyTable is the pair alternative to RoundTable. Pairs share a common piece of paper, which they hand back and forth, each contributing in turn. Science examples to use Rallytable might be: "Come up with a list of everything you know about spiders, taking turns writing each fact." Or, "Write a paragraph on what you know about spiders, taking turns writing each sentence."

Structure 10

RoundRobin

Each student, in turn, shares with teammates. Roundrobin is an easy way to have students share any information with teammates in a format that ensures equal participation.

RoundRobin is simply speaking in turn within teams. For example, students can share how they feel about space exploration or can read their papers on space exploration to teammates. Many conditions can be attached to RoundRobin to make it achieve the results desired. For example, each person must speak for thirty seconds and no longer; or each person must quickly paraphrase (or praise) the previous person's comments before making their own; or each person must offer something new to the RoundRobin.

RoundTable

In teams, students take turns writing. Roundtable is a great way to generate a list of ideas or to write team papers. The turn-taking ensures equal participation.

RoundTable is a written RoundRobin. Ideas, answers, or any type of contribution is made as the paper is passed around the table. RoundTable is an excellent structure for brainstorming and generating lists, especially if it is done quickly. For example, "List as many elements as you can." RoundTable also works well for writing as a team. Each student must participate in the team writing task. For example, "Write a brief description of the Periodic Table. Take turns writing each sentence."

Virginia DeBolt: *Write! Social Studies*
Kagan Publishing • 1 (800) 933-2667

119

Structure 12

Teams Post

A representative from each team simultaneously records the team's answer or idea on the chalkboard to share with the class. Teams Post promotes information sharing among teams while saving valuable time.

Just as students benefit from sharing questions, answers and ideas within teams, teams can benefit by sharing with other teams. Teams can build on each other's ideas; an idea shared may trigger a whole new direction for exploration or spark new ideas for discussion. A representative from each team simultaneously records the team's answer or idea on a designated area of the chalkboard. Representatives can be team selected, or you can select each team's representative by announcing a student number, "Student Threes, please record your team's answer on the chalkboard." In a brief amount of time and with little interruption to the teamwork, all teams have access to each other's ideas or answers.

Structure 13

Stand-N-Share

Students stand to share their ideas with the class. Students sit when a similar idea has been shared. Stand-N-Share is a quick an easy way to share ideas with the entire class.

In Stand-N-Share, teams discuss an idea or issue until each person feels he or she could share an important point with the class. The team stands up. When all the teams are standing, the teacher asks one student to share with the class. After hearing what the first student says, any others who planned to share the same idea or a similar one sit down. Another standing student is called on to share with the class. The process repeats until all students are seated. In a brief time, every point on the topic can be shared.

Virginia DeBolt: *Write! Social Studies*
Kagan Publishing • 1 (800) 933-2667

Structure 14

Team Discussion

Students discuss any topic as a team. Team Discussion is a simple, unstructured platform for students to share their ideas with teammates.

The teacher announces the topic to discuss. Discussion topics are usually open-ended with no right or wrong answers. For example, "Who is the most important mathematician?" Following the Team Discussion, select one student from several teams share their ideas with the entire class.

Structure 15

Team Interview

Students on each team are interviewed, in turn, by teammates. Team Interview is a great way for students to share with teammates and to probe teammates for information.

In Team Interview, one student on the team is selected to go first. He or she stands up. Teammates have a predetermined amount of time to ask him or her questions to learn as much as they can about the topic. When the time is up, the next student stands, and teammates pump him or her for information.

A simple variation is to have students present information to teammates first, then teammates may ask additional questions.

Virginia DeBolt: *Write! Social Studies*
Kagan Publishing • 1 (800) 933-2667

121

Team Project

Students work together as a team to complete a team project. Team Projects provide students a great deal of autonomy as they work cooperatively toward a common goal.

The teacher announces the team project. Each team may have a unique project or all teams may work on the same project. Projects can involve any type of teamwork: creating products, doing research, solving problems, composing a song, conducting experiments, coordinating a dance or movement. Without any structure, students may run into complications with a project. One or two students may do all of the work while the others do not contribute at all. To avoid this pitfall, try one or more of the following ideas:

• **Assign Roles**—Assign each student a role specific to the project. As a class, brainstorm and have students record "Things to Do" and "Things to Say" to fulfill each role. Some generic roles you may use include: Checker, Cheerleader, Coach, Encourager, Gatekeeper, Materials Monitor, Praiser, Question Commander, Quiet Captain, Recorder, Reflector, Taskmaster.

• **Divide the Work**—Divide the work of the project or have students divide the work so that everyone must participate.

• **Limit the Resources**—By limiting who can use which resources, students depend on each other for completing the project.

• **Individual Papers or Tests**—Have students each turn in their own paper on the topic or be responsible for their own learning. Do not use group grades for team projects.

Virginia DeBolt: *Write! Social Studies*
Kagan Publishing • 1 (800) 933-2667

Teams Present

Teams share their project with another team or with the class. Teams Present is a great way to practice presentation skills and disseminate information.

Following an activity or project in which the teams have worked to make a product or demonstrate an idea, have them present their work to another team or to the class. Presenting to one other team has the advantage of more active participation and a distinct time advantage. For each team to do a five-minute presentation to the class, with eight teams would take about 40 minutes. Of the 40 minutes, students are active presenters for five minutes and passive viewers for 35 minutes. Teams can present to one other team and watch one other team's five-minute presentation in just 10 minutes, during all of which they are active presenters or viewers. In the same amount of time as a class presentation, teams can share their presentation and view one other team's presentation four times. Repeated practice allows students the opportunity to hone their presentation skills. Presenting to the whole class has the advantage of a larger audience and the advantage of every student getting the opportunity to see every team's presentation.

Regardless of whether students present to one other team, to several teams, or to the whole class, it is still important to make sure each student is individually accountable for his or her own contribution. Students can be held accountable by each presenting part of the information, turning in a paper on the presentation, or being held responsible for all material in the presentation.

Virginia DeBolt: *Write! Social Studies*
Kagan Publishing • 1 (800) 933-2667

123

Structure 18

ThinkPad Brainstorming

Students generate a number of ideas on a given topic, each on a separate thinkpad slip and share their ideas with teammates. ThinkPad Brainstorming promotes creative thinking.

In ThinkPad Brainstorming, students work individually, recording their brainstormed ideas on thinkpad slips, small sheets of paper or cards. After a period of time or after students have generated enough ideas on a topic, students share their ideas in a RoundRobin. Teammates work together to see if they can build on ideas generated or come up with new and even better ideas. The ideas that are generated can be easily sorted and categorized. See Team Sort.

Virginia DeBolt: *Write! Social Studies*
Kagan Publishing • 1 (800) 933-2667

Think-Pair-Share

After a question or topic is announced by the teacher, students "Think" about the question, "Pair" up with a partner to discuss the question, then some students are selected to "Share" their ideas with the class. Think-Pair-Share is a simple and powerful technique for developing and sharing ideas.

The teacher poses a question for the class to think about. Think-Pair-Share works best with low-consensus, thinking questions to which there is not a right or wrong answer. For example, some questions to spark some interest on endangered species: "Some species are threatened with extinction. Should we let natural selection run its course, or should we intervene?" "What are some things we could do to help protect the bald eagle?" Give students a good 10-15 seconds of think time. Then, have students pair up with another student on their team to share what they think. After students have shared their ideas, select a few students to share with the class their ideas, or their partner's ideas. Think-Pair-Share can be used several times in succession to follow a line of reasoning or more fully develop a concept with interrelated issues. Have students pair up with a different teammate with each new question.

1. Think

2. Pair

3. Share

Virginia DeBolt: *Write! Social Studies*
Kagan Publishing • 1 (800) 933-2667

125

Structure 20

Think-Pair-Write

In this variation of Think-Pair-Share, instead of selecting a few students to share their ideas with the class after the think and pair discussion time, have all students write down their ideas. Think-Pair-Write is an excellent way to prime the writing pump.

Think-Pair-Write substitutes a writing component for Think-Pair-Share's last step, sharing with the class. After the think time and pair discussion, students write down their own ideas, the ideas their partner shared, or even new ideas. Students can do a number of Think-Pair-Writes in succession to discuss and develop ideas on the topic. For a fresh perspective on the same topic, repeat the question and have students pair with a new teammate. Think-Pair-Write is a great way to pique students' interest in a topic and is an excellent prewriting activity. After several rounds of Think-Pair-Write, students will have discussed the topic in detail and developed a set of notes which they may use for the basis of writing on the topic.

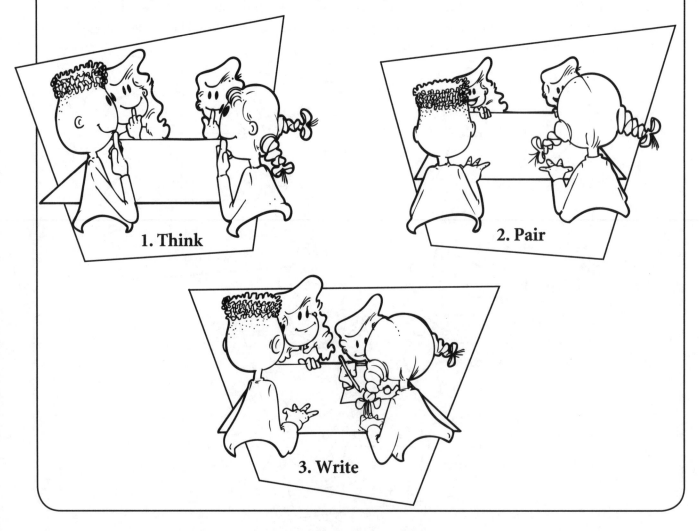

1. Think

2. Pair

3. Write

Virginia DeBolt: *Write! Social Studies*
Kagan Publishing • 1 (800) 933-2667

Think-Write-Pair

In Think-Write-Pair, students write down their own ideas before they pair up to discuss them with a partner. Think-Write-Pair allows students to more fully develop their own ideas before sharing them.

After the think time, students write down their own ideas. This allows more reflective students and students who develop their thinking through writing explore the question or issue in more detail before they are asked to share their ideas with a partner. When students pair up, they read what they wrote to their partner, then discuss the issue more. The added writing component often leads to a richer pair discussion.

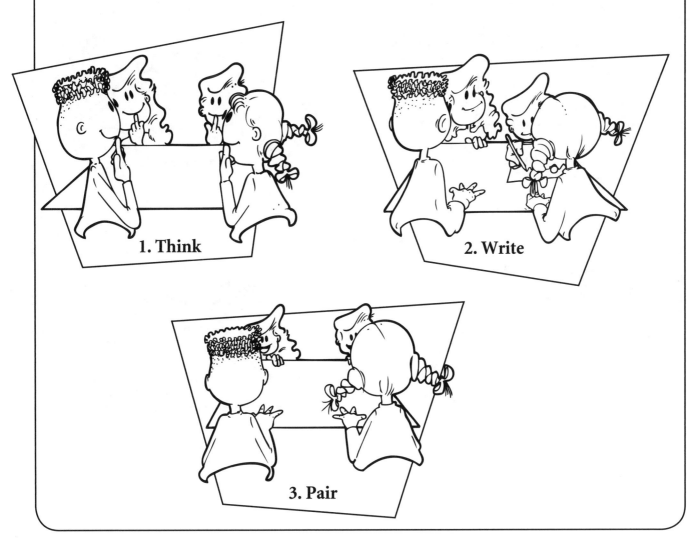

1. Think

2. Write

3. Pair

Virginia DeBolt: *Write! Social Studies*
Kagan Publishing • 1 (800) 933-2667

127

Think-Write-Pair-Square

This structure is the same as Think-Write-Pair, except as a final step, pairs pair up to form a foursome to discuss the topic.

The teacher announces a topic and gives students time to think about the topic. Students write their ideas down and then pair up to discuss their ideas. Pairs pair up to form a team of four. The foursome discusses their ideas on the topic.

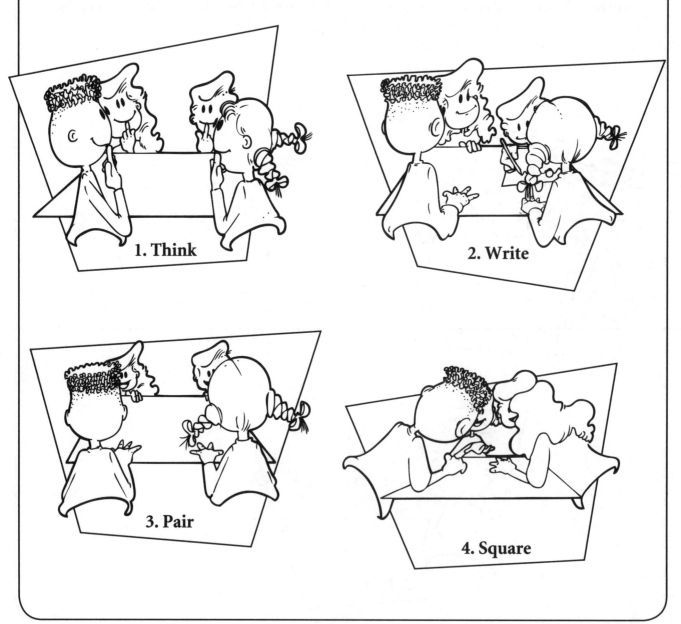

1. Think

2. Write

3. Pair

4. Square

Virginia DeBolt: *Write! Social Studies*
Kagan Publishing • 1 (800) 933-2667

Value Lines

Students line up on an imaginary line according to their agreement or disagreement with a value statement. Value lines is a good way to get students personally involved in the learning and explore students values relating to an issue.

The teacher poses a value statement and frames it in a way that students may agree with or disagree with the statement. Some social studies examples: "We should institute a death penalty." Or, "Presidents should have not have term limits." Students get out of their seats and line up according to their agreement or disagreement with the statement. Students who strongly agree go to one end of the line, students who strongly disagree to the other end, and uncommitted students line up in the middle. Students are asked to pair up with a partner next to them to discuss their stance on the issue. Then, the line may be folded so students who strongly agree may discuss their point of view with students who strongly disagree. The line may also be split in the middle, and slid so students who do not feel strongly about the issue get the opportunity to discuss the issue with students who are adamant.

Agree ← Ⓐ ◯ ◯ ◯ ? ? ◯ ◯ ◯ Ⓓ → **Disagree**

Virginia DeBolt: *Write! Social Studies*
Kagan Publishing • 1 (800) 933-2667

129

Bibliography

Bantock, Nick. *Griffin and Sabine, An Extraordinary Correspondence.* Chronicle Books, San Francisco, CA, 1991.

Bantock, Nick. *Sabine's Notebook.* Chronicle Books, San Francisco, CA, 1992.

Bantock, Nick. *The Golden Mean.* Chronicle Books, San Francisco, CA, 1993.

Bloom, Benjamin S., et al. *A Taxonomy of Educational Objectives: Handbook 1: Cognitive Domain.* Longman, New York, 1977.

Campbell, Linda, et al. *Teaching and Learning Through Multiple Intelligences.* New Horizons for Learning, Stanwood, WA, 1992.

DeBolt, Virginia. *Write! Cooperative Learning and the Writing Process.* Kagan Publishing, San Clemente, CA, 1994.

Dickson, Paul. *Timelines.* Addison-Wesley Publishing, Reading, MA, 1990.

Gere, Anne Ruggles, ed. *Roots in the Sawdust: Writing to Learn across the Disciplines.* National Council of Teachers of English, Urbana, IL, 1985.

Kagan, Laurie, Kagan, Miguel and Kagan Spencer. *Teambuilding.* Kagan Publishing, San Clemente, CA, 1997.

Kagan, Miguel, Robertson, Laurie and Kagan, Spencer. *Classbuilding.* Kagan Publishing, San Clemente, CA, 1995.

Kagan, Spencer. *Kagan Cooperative Learning.* Kagan Publishing, San Clemente, CA, 2009.

Kagan, Spencer and Kagan, Miguel. *Advanced Cooperative Learning: Playing with Elements.* Kagan Publishing, San Clemente, CA, 1994.

Kagan, Spencer and Kagan, Miguel. *Multiple Intelligences: Teaching With, For, and About MI.* Kagan Publishing, San Clemente, CA, 1998.

Virginia DeBolt: *Write! Social Studies*
Kagan Publishing • 1 (800) 933-2667

131

Bibliography (cont)

Parks, Sandra and Black, Howard. *Organizing Thinking: Graphic Organizers.* Critical Thinking Press and Software, Pacific Grove, CA, 1992.

Shaw, Vanston. *Communitybuilding.* Kagan Publishing, San Clemente, CA, 1992.

Tompkins, Gale. *Teaching Writing: Balancing Process and Product.* Macmillan, New York, 1994.

Zinsser, William. *On Writing Well: An Informal Guide to Writing Nonfiction.* Harper Perennial, New York, 1994.

132

Virginia DeBolt: *Write! Social Studies*
Kagan Publishing • 1 (800) 933-2667

About the Author

Virginia DeBolt has been teaching for thirty years in Colorado, New Mexico and Texas. She is currently teaching English at Murchison Middle School in Austin, Texas. She has worked with all ages from kindergarten to adult, but enjoys most the opportunity to work with other teachers and share ideas about writing and cooperative learning. She is interested in publishing students' writing on the internet and is creating a web home page for her school. Her personal home page can be viewed at http://www.flash.net/~vdebolt.

More Books by Virginia

Write! Cooperative Learning and the Writing Process

Three methods to make your students better writers: Have them 1) Write! 2) Write! and 3) Write some more. You receive ready-to-use writing lessons in each of the writing domains: imaginative, functional, communication, non-fiction/reporting, and opinion making. Cooperative learning structures are used at each of the stages of the writing process: prewriting, writing, proofing and editing, conferring and rewriting, and publishing. Includes practical management tips, references, resources, and ideas for evaluating students' writing with portfolios, holistic scoring, primary trait scoring, analytic, self evaluation, and peer evaluation.

Write! Across the Curriculum Book Series

Move beyond drill and kill. Teach for understanding. Integrate writing across the curriculum! When students write in science, social studies and mathematics, they delve deeply into content and issues, their thinking is clarified and they obtain a deeper understanding and appreciation for the content. Writing makes the content accessible to your verbal/Linguistic students. Each book includes 36 multiple intelligences, cooperative writing activities with ready-to-use reproducible activity pages, and a brief description of dozens of strategies. Teammates work cooperatively on these writing activities. Writing activities are a perfect way to start the class, introduce a new concept, end the unit, or use as a sponge activity.

Write! Mathematics

Includes activities like writing the steps of solving a problem, composing word problems, restating definitions, and translating the language of math

Write! Science

Includes activities like keeping a science log, defining science concepts, writing how something works, prioritizing world problems, coming up with a new invention.

Write! Social Studies

Includes activities like writing the correspondence of two historical characters, publishing and sharing political cartoons, discussing and writing about famous historical quotations.

Available from Kagan Publishing

Virginia DeBolt: *Write! Social Studies*
Kagan Publishing • 1 (800) 933-2667

133

Note Page

Virginia DeBolt: *Write! Social Studies*
Kagan Publishing • 1 (800) 933-2667

Note Page

Virginia DeBolt: *Write! Social Studies*
Kagan Publishing • 1 (800) 933-2667

135

Note Page

Virginia DeBolt: *Write! Social Studies*
Kagan Publishing • 1 (800) 933-2667